CAROL
LaCHAPELLE

FINDING YOUR VOICE TELLING YOUR STORIES

167 Ways to Tell Your Life Stories

Marion Street Press, Inc.
Oak Park, Illinois

Cover design by Rick Menard

ISBN 13: 978-1-933338-32-3
Printed in U.S.A.
Printing 10 9 8 7 6 5 4 3 2 1

Marion Street Press, Inc.
PO Box 2249
Oak Park, IL 60303
www.marionstreetpress.com

Carol LaChapelle is a Chicago-based writer and writing coach who specializes in helping people tell their stories--whether for themselves in a personal journal, for family histories, or as published memoirs. For the past 20 years, she has offered her workshops for healthcare professionals; therapists and counselors; educators and clergy; various support groups; and the general public. She welcomes contact with readers through her website www.carollachapelle.com or her email, madmoon55@hotmail.com.

Contents

PREFACE

I'm not sure when I first became obsessed with stories, though I was an early and avid reader of familiar childhood tales: Peter Pan and Tinker Bell, Hansel and Gretel, even the sad Little Match Girl. Through these characters and their adventures, I'd find not only entertainment and escape, but also connection and comfort. What's more, though these characters seemed both like and unlike me, their stories illuminated something about my own.

And these reasons for loving stories are true for me still. When I meet someone, the first thing I want to know is his or her story. Who are you? Where do you come from? What is your life like? My friends kid me about how I "interview" people, but all I'm really asking for are their stories.

An illustration: In 1998, I conducted a journal writing workshop at a conference of religious activists in Milwaukee. At dinner that night, I was seated with some of the attendees, all strangers to me. As is true in those settings, most of our table talk was benign, pleasant, and boring. Then, in response to one of my "interview" questions, the man seated next to me revealed that his 21-year-old son had just come out as a gay man. Suddenly I perked up, interested in how this gentle and caring father from the heartland was going to negotiate this dramatic turn of events in his life. Now our interaction, minutes ago so superficial, had the potential for real contact, for genuine human connection. That is the power of story.

While human beings have always told each other stories, modern life has pushed this practice to the margins. Most people no longer keep diaries or write letters. Few of us linger at the kitchen table to tell family stories. We have less access to the keepers of our generational stories—our grandparents, aunts and uncles. (There is an African proverb that says when an elder dies, an entire library is lost.) And while as a culture we are encouraged to consume the stories of others—in films and books, on TV and in the tabloids—few ordinary people find opportunities for producing their own stories.

But fortunately that is changing. There has been a resurgence in personal storytelling, and in some very interesting places. Oral history projects like StoryCorp travel the nation inviting citizens to record their stories. The National Endowment of the Arts began in 2004 to offer writing workshops to help men and women in the military—and their friends and family—tell their stories. Medical schools now train doctors to better listen to their patients' stories. Memoirs and autobiographies top best seller lists, and libraries, even historical societies, regularly hold courses in genealogy and life writing.

My personal love of stories merged with the professional in 1992, when I was asked to teach a course at Chicago's Field Museum of Natural History as part of Women's History month.

I chose the book, *We Are the Stories We Tell* (ed. Wendy Martin). Still in print, it is an anthology of short stories, with one memoir piece by Mary McCarthy. Close to 15 women showed up for the course—ranging in age from 16 to 82—all eager to discuss the readings, but more important, as it turned out, to share their own personal stories.

It was thrilling to watch this group of strangers quickly cohere through the process of storytelling. It didn't matter that they were from different generations, ethnic groups, educational and professional backgrounds. When they told their stories, they were immediately connected by all the shared human drama of birth and death, love and loss, adventure, regret, and triumph.

The course of my own teaching was inexorably set during that experience. I opted out of the academic life and began offering writing workshops in continuing education and professional development venues, including libraries, hospitals, community colleges, and churches, and for support groups. Over these past 16 years, I've been privileged to work with people of all ages and backgrounds, each with a story to tell, whether for themselves in a private journal; in collected family histories, letters, and diaries; or for publication.

At the heart of this work are the close to 200 writing prompts I've created to lead people in my workshops back to the significant people, places, and events in their lives. Over the years, these same students have urged me to collect these exercises into a book. And so I have.

Finding Your Voice, Telling Your Stories, as I hope you'll discover, benefits greatly from the feedback these real users have given me. In truth, my students' footprints are all over this book. I couldn't have done it without them.

Introduction

Why Tell Our Stories?

It might have happened something like this: Sitting around the campfire on a cool summer night, recovering from the rigors of the day's hunt, one of our earliest ancestors, Thor, begins to recount for all assembled the details of the harrowing event: how the hunting party took the path nearest the river; how they cornered and killed the animal; how they carried it back to camp.

In the process of passing along this vital information, and while attempting to instruct his listeners on what makes for a successful hunt, Thor notices that his audience's attention is starting to wane—so much detail, all those important facts piling up in no particular order. How was anyone supposed to remember it all?

So our ancestor-raconteur starts over, making sure to describe the experience in sequence, and builds slowly to the Big Moment. He tells how the hunting party started out that morning, adding some details about the weather, the smell of the early rain, the hopeful sense of anticipation among the men. Then he describes what they saw and heard along the way: the multicolored birds that sounded "like this"; the big slow-moving insects on the ground; the size of the horns on the large animal who suddenly charged them.

Our ancestor sees that his audience is now paying closer attention, a sense of anticipation playing across their faces. And so his description of the ensuing action—their vanquishing of that animal whose very bones now lay scattered around the cave floor—starts to get a little more detailed, more dramatic. In the process, his facial expressions begin to mimic the earlier terror they'd all felt. Then he stands, broadening his shoulders, and shows the rapt audience how in spite of their fear, the hunters stood their ground against the beast.

And as he reaches that climactic moment to which all his telling has been directed, our ancestor's listeners—the men, women, and children gathered around the dying embers—vigorously nod their heads in approval, clap their hands together, the image of the slain beast and the victorious hunting party now burned into their collective memories.

And so was born the story.

~

We know that human beings across time and place have always told stories. These patterned structures for recounting our experience are the form in which we best learn how to get on in the world; they hold our attention as the important lessons come pouring in. Stories also help us frame, contain, and make sense of our experience, they teach us about ourselves and the world we live in. On this most elemental level, we tell stories to survive, even thrive.

Here are just some of the ways stories work to do this:

Stories Entertain Us

No matter the content or tone of a story—happy, scary, or sad—it's enjoyable to hear and read stories. Our brains light up in all the right places and suddenly we've entered another world, another's sensibility and experience. Perhaps that is at the root of being entertained: we leave the ordinary for the duration of a story and inhabit the imagined. Maybe like sleep and dreams, stories give us respite from our own nattering minds and troubling lives.

Years ago, about to have surgery for an early cancer, I couldn't stop thinking about my situation. I barely ate, couldn't sleep, couldn't keep the anxiety at bay for more than minutes at a time. Then one night I began reading Thomas Harris' *Red Dragon*, the precursor to *The Silence of the Lambs*. I'll be forever grateful to that author; for those few hours, this terrifying story gave me temporary escape from real terror.

Stories Help Us Remember

See above. I remember the details from that time in my life because I just told a story about it—albeit a brief and undeveloped one. I remember the name of the book, the one that followed it, the author, and even the room where I read it. I could also describe how skinny I got from not eating and smoking too much, the brown leather boots I wore to a party just a week before the surgery, and the guy I went to the party with—yes, him, the shy, balding vegetarian. Current research about how memory works supports this idea that we remember things better when we tell stories about them. Narrative is the frame onto which we organize the random details of our experience, and so better remember those details.

Stories particularly help us remember those people who are no longer living. I noted in my journal on the 33rd anniversary of my mother's death—at the too-young age of 50—that people die twice: when they physically die, and when we stop telling stories about them. "We cannot keep her alive," I wrote about my mother on May 13, 1997, "if we stop telling stories about her."

STORIES TEACH US

Some stories teach us real things, like how to make a quilt, run the Iditarod, or travel the Orient Express. Mostly, though, stories teach us the *really* real things: how to survive great loss; fight our way back from failure; forgive our transgressors and move on; and keep a sense of magic in our lives. I need reminders about the latter because like most people I too often go on automatic pilot, getting trapped on the tedium treadmill. When that happens, I'll look for a good story to snap me out of it.

And telling our own stories can be doubly instructive. As we write them down—and regularly re-read them—the meaning and significance of our life is revealed: What and who matters to us? What have we learned about ourselves and the world we inhabit? How can we keep from repeating mistakes? And most important, where do our stories go from here? In this sense, knowing our story helps us take authorship of our lives.

STORIES INSPIRE US

Simon Ortiz, the American Indian poet and writer said, "There are no truths, only stories." This probably unnerves some people who believe in immutable truths, but for me this quote *is* an immutable truth. When we hear someone's story, something shifts in us, opens up, no matter how certain we were of a truth before hearing it.

In the late '70s, following our country's withdrawal from Vietnam, two friends and I volunteered to sponsor a Vietnamese boat family—refugees from that country's long history of war—for resettlement in Chicago's infamous Uptown, long an established port of entry for immigrants. Our particular family was made up of the mother and father—he a practicing Chinese herbalist, a profession that made them firmly middle class in their own country—and their 14 children ranging in age from eight to 18.

My favorite stories about this sponsorship fall into two categories: how I and my friends made this family's transition a little easier, and how each family member—from little eight-year-old Hue to the frail but stoic patriarch—taught us a lot about courage, the strength of community, and the all-too-cliched value of hard work. No job—no matter the hours, the pay, the drudgery—was beneath them. They simply did what they had to do to survive, and were grateful beyond imagining for the opportunity. Within six months of their arrival on the mean streets of Chicago, this family and its collective wage earners had saved enough money—in cash—to buy a used car and drive to California for vacation. Ah, the American dream!

But more, having been part of this family's story, I can never again assume anything about anyone solely from her external circumstances: where she's from, what she looks like, how she dresses or speaks, or the work she does. Once I know her story, we make a connection.

Stories Connect Us

Yes, stories connect us—to other people, to our own past, even to the future. When my great-niece Nell was three years old, she said to me one day with great enthusiasm, "Remember my birthday party??? When all my people were there?? It was a wonderful time!!"

And for her the wonderfulness was not only in the boatload of presents she received, but in being surrounded by "her people"—her parents, grandparents, aunts, uncles, and cousins who regularly provide her with the safety and security she needs to grow and prosper. All of these people—and their stories—provide the context within which her identity will be formed, a self that is both connected to and separate from "her people."

Finally, Stories Save Us

We seem to particularly need stories during times of great sorrow and loss. I remember how my father, brother and I kept telling each other the story of my mother's illness and death—both during and after the event. There was something immensely soothing in that process: the way we repeated each important detail, the sense that we were containing our loss through the ordered recounting of the experience. The telling and re-telling of that story also served as catharsis—we could cry, laugh, get angry, get mad, feel sad over and over again. Telling sorrowful stories is a necessary part of the healing process.

And when we share these stories with others, they might be inspired to persist in the face of adversity, to believe in their own capacity to survive trauma and loss. This is surely one of the powerful uses of story, one that has worked in so many ways in my own life.

In the end, telling stories is perhaps the most human thing we do. They teach us who we are and where we've come from; they anchor and connect us to each other; they guide us through both good and bad times. In all these ways and more, stories—no less than food and love—sustain us as we go about creating a meaningful life.

Chapter 1

How to Use This Book

The following suggestions were developed over the years in response to questions from students in my workshops. Because they originate in people's direct experience with the writing exercises, the answers should help you get the most out of this book.

As you make your way through the exercises in this book, you'll find that there is an overlap among them. People exercises will often lead to place stories, and vice versa. Recalling specific events may be a way into a story topic. This is a natural result of the writing process, which is always one of discovery. So go to where the writing is leading you. You needn't feel wedded to the story you start out to tell; instead be open to the story that's waiting to be told.

There is no set order or schedule to the writing exercises. Start anywhere and go to any other set of exercises, or to another exercise within the same group. You can even return to the same exercise months or years later and discover something new from it.

Do as many exercises at one sitting, and write as many times a week or month, as you'd like, though I recommend a minimum frequency of once every three to four weeks. Such regularity will make the practice of writing down your stories much more satisfying and rewarding. It will also help you get in the habit of telling your current and future stories.

One of the most frequently asked questions in my memoir writing workshops is: Should we handwrite our stories or use a computer? While ultimately a matter of preference, I always come down on the side of handwriting. For many people, paper and pens are still more portable than computers. I carry my journal and write everywhere I go—on buses, trains and planes, in waiting rooms, while sitting in coffeehouses and bookstores. But maybe the most important reason to handwrite is the process itself: the movement of our hand across the page, combined with the way the eye tracks the words as they're written, actually changes the way we think, creating synaptic leaps and links that lead us to new images, new memories, and new revelations. I handwrite, too, because my own peculiar scrawl and scribbles visually reflect my thoughts and images—and the emotions they arouse—not those of just any Times Roman user. Having said that, I definitely promote the PC for its ease in editing. If you want a printed version of your stories, the computer is an indispensable tool.

What kind of writing journal you use is your own choice. I generally make no recommendations as to size, color, number of pages, lined or unlined. I purposefully made ***Finding Your Voice*** a guide and not a workbook with lots of empty pages following each exercise. I myself never buy those books. They are someone else's idea of what my journal should look like. I favor simple lined notebooks, not too big or fancy. But if you like large blank sketch books with sequined covers, then that's what you should use. And if you're not sure which style, size, or color suits you, just linger awhile in the stationery aisle of bookstores, art supply stores, or your local drugstore. Pick up and handle a bunch of notebooks, then choose whichever one feels right.

Even though you'll be recording experiences from the past, including the recent past, try using the present tense when doing some of the exercises. For instance, "I am standing in the library when suddenly...." "We board the plane and begin the adventure of a lifetime." "He raced in the door and announced...." And so on. The immediacy of the present tense will put you fully in the scene you want to describe or story you want to tell. When that happens, you may better recall what you saw, heard, smelled, tasted or touched. Those sensual details are more likely to lead you to those memories worth recording—and re-reading.

At first glance, some of these exercises might not seem to apply to you. Maybe you didn't have pets while growing up, didn't go to college, or didn't live in a traditional family. But I encourage you not to skip over them; instead consider each of the writing prompts that follow. You might find they stir a memory or two.

When doing these exercises, you will variously recall single images, whole scenes, or complete stories. The major difference among these is that entire stories, whether they occur over the course of a day or a decade, usually involve an event, conflict, problem, or dramatic encounter that gets explained or resolved by the story's end. There is a recognizable beginning, middle, and end in stories, and usually a change, revelation, or discovery by the main character(s). This is not always true of images and scenes, many of which capture moments of experience or bursts of spontaneous emotion. Still, each type of memory recall is valuable, and will lead you to a deeper appreciation of the richness of your life.

The exercises in this book are designed so that you can return to them again and again, always finding more to write about. There is no expiration date on this book; it will stay fresh for as long as you have stories to tell.

In addition to your own recall, you might want to use your or others' diaries, letters, e-mails, even photographs to trigger your memories. Or you might ask family and friends about certain experiences or times you shared together. I'm always amazed (and a bit chagrined) by how much my lifelong friend Judy remembers about our high school and college days. When she starts telling those stories, it brings back people, places, and events I thought long lost to me.

The poet Anne Sexton wrote, "It doesn't matter who my father was; it matters who I remember he was." The more we know about how memory works—and the study of memory is a hot research topic these days—the better we understand that our memories are not fixed or static, like a photograph capturing a factual rendering of "reality." (But is even that true?

Certainly there is an editorial process at work when selecting what gets left in or out of a photo.)

Our memories are fluid; we construct and re-construct them, changing them even as we retrieve and record them, influenced in large part by what we are feeling at the time. Given this, my advice is to stay true to your feelings, to your felt sense as you unearth and record your memories. You're not lying or inventing when you do this—as novelists might, making up whole characters, places, or events. Instead you are being faithful to your emotional experience of events, giving an emotionally accurate account of what happened, and what it felt like for you to be there.

If you've lived a full life, most likely you've lived a life full of hurt, sadness, failure, disappointment, and loss—perhaps even of true tragedy. And so when you tell certain stories, these feelings may re-emerge. Why enter this often disturbing territory again?

I think we do so because we believe that telling our stories can help us transcend, and, to some degree, move beyond painful experiences; this may be one of the reasons human beings are hard-wired for narrative. When we recount such memories in story form—especially in writing—we gain a certain distance from them, a perspective, our point of view is altered and broadened, important insights are revealed.

Telling stories also helps us gain mastery over painful experiences. We do this by bearing witness: the quiet, courageous act of speaking our truth and in our own voice. ("Listen," we write, "this is what it was like for me.") There is power in that voice; when we see it expressed on the page, our bad and sad stories may start to lose their hold on us. So while we may never completely overcome the damaging consequences of some of our experiences, telling our stories about them can help move us through them, becoming stronger as a result of having survived. As Hemingway wrote, "The world breaks everyone, and afterwards, many are strong at the broken places."

And should you choose to share some of your triumph-over-adversity stories, know that they will inspire and give hope to others. Whenever I hit some wall in my life, I know that a story from someone who's been there—and lived "to tell the tale"—will give me the needed courage and tenacity to carry on.

Please note: Each of us is the final authority on when or even if we tell certain of our stories. With that in mind, I am pleased to pass along an important rule, The Flip-Out Rule, with the gracious consent of its author James W. Pennebaker, professor and chair of psychology at the University of Texas at Austin. When I first read the Rule in Dr. Pennebaker's book, *Writing To Heal* (New Harbinger Publications, 2004), I knew it would make an important addition to this guide. Here it is:

"If you feel that your writing about a particular topic is too much for you to handle, then do not write about it. If you know that you aren't ready to address a particularly painful topic, write about something else. When you are ready, then tackle it. If you feel that you will flip out by writing, don't write."

In her essay "Memory & Imagination," memoirist Patricia Hampl writes that we learn not only to tell our stories, but to listen to what our stories tell us: This happened, but what does it mean? That is the human endeavor, after all—to make sense of things, to seek pattern and meaning in our life experiences. So as you write down your stories, be open to what you discover in the process—about yourself, other people, those big events and small moments that make up a life.

As you write your stories, be aware that you are the first and only reader of them. If you decide to share your stories at some point, you'll want to revise and edit them for another reader. But it is important that you remain the sole reader of your writing until you choose otherwise. Only then will you be less tempted to censor yourself or be critical of how or what you write.

The title of this book could as easily have been *Telling Your Stories, Finding Your Voice* as *Finding Your Voice, Telling Your Stories*. They are, after all, mutually reinforcing activities. The more we find our voice—hear our authentic self expressed on the page—the more willing we are to tell our stories. And the more we tell our stories, the clearer and truer our voice will sound. And that's what it all hinges on: telling the truth. Tell your stories true, and you'll find your true voice. Find your true voice, and you'll find the truth in your stories.

Finally, I am fortunate that so many of my workshop students responded to my call to submit their own stories for inclusion in this book. You'll find their contributions in the *From the Trenches* section following many of the writing exercises. I am grateful for the time and effort they took to be a part of *Finding Your Voice, Telling Your Stories*.

Chapter 2

FOUR REALLY HELPFUL WRITING TECHNIQUES

When I first started teaching memoir writing 16 years ago, I wanted to design exercises that would help people, especially non-writers, more easily recall their life stories. I'd attended too many workshops where the facilitator said, "OK, now write about an important childhood memory," then fail to give further instructions. Where to begin, I'd wonder? How to pick and choose among the endless possibilities? How to even find those possibilities, many of which were hidden deep in my memory. Such a broad, general exercise left me—a lifelong journal keeper and writer—struggling to begin. And as I looked around the room, I knew I wasn't alone.

So in my own workshops, I wanted my students to have a clear way back into their stories, a series of roadmaps leading to the significant people, places, and events in their lives. These maps consist of specific writing techniques, each giving us a place to begin on the blank page.

When we start a writing exercise with a technique—the list, freewrite, description, or character sketch—we allow the magic of writing to take over and take us back to those memories we thought lost forever.

Over time we learn to trust the process, to face the blank page not with reluctance or anxiety, but with knowledge born of experience. We begin to write, the words spill out of our pen, soon leading us to images. These images pull us deeper into our memory, into whole scenes, and finally full stories. It can and will happen again and again once we start writing. The following techniques will help you begin writing, stay writing, and discover your stories.

1. The List

The list is the starter technique for many of the writing exercises in this book; it's an easy, user-friendly way to begin. When making a list, you simply jot down in no particular order whatever words or brief phrases are inspired by the list's subject heading. Here's a great list exercise to practice with, one that will help you tell your current stories.

Head the list "Significant Events" and begin to make a list of those important or significant experiences from the past week. Include experiences from work, hobbies and avocations, and your social and personal life. These can be positive or negative experiences, big or small ones, just so long as you deem them important. As you make this list, ask yourself which interactions, conversations, people and places from just this one week in your life were significant. (NOTE: For this exercise, do not rely on calendars or date books to jog your memory; rather, see what bubbles up without any external prompting.)

After you make the list, circle the three most important or noteworthy entries, then choose one to write about. This should be the most important thing that happened to you during the past week, for whatever reason. (And you might be surprised at what you select.)

Tell the story of this experience. Be sure to include setting—where and when it happened; the characters—who was involved other than yourself; and the action—what happened. And if there's any interesting dialogue you can recall, include it. In the process of recording this experience, see how its meaning or significance is revealed. In other words, what do you come to understand about yourself, another person, or the world at large in telling this story?

A note about lists: The greatest benefit of the list technique is the profusion of writing exercises it can generate. Over time, you can write about every entry on your lists—and keep adding to them as well. That's why this technique is one of the most productive in the book; it guarantees you enough stories to tell for a very long time.

2. Focused Freewriting

Freewriting is a kind of automatic writing. You write fast, for 10 minutes, without stopping. Your goal is to let words pour onto the page in no particular order. When freewriting, you don't stop to correct spelling or grammar; you don't edit or even finish a sentence if you don't want to. This technique pushes you to give up control of the writing and to follow it instead. This can feel risky at times, as you may not always like the direction the writing is taking, especially if it starts to reveal something true but unpleasant. Yet the truth is usually where the energy is in your writing. Discovering that truth is the main reason we tell stories in the first place.

Several years ago, I hit a wall while writing an essay about the absence of wild animals in large urban areas. I was half way into it when the writing began turning to mush. I knew there was nothing to do but leave it alone, so I got up from my desk and took my journal into another room. I sat in my most comfortable chair and began freewriting, using the word "animals" as the focus. Then minutes into the exercise, I'd unearthed a memory of my young mother, a story that passed into family legend even while it was happening:

She's driving alone down a dimly lit suburban road, on her way home from her weekly bowling night, when suddenly she sees a small cat fall into an open manhole. Horrified, she stops and jumps out of the car. Kneeling at the lip of the dark open space, my mother lifts the terrified animal out of the hole, a mewling, scraggly cat who will go on to become "Stranger," the latest addition to our domestic menagerie.

But instead of being elated at this buried memory, I was frustrated at the turn the writing had taken — how did that image possibly connect to my essay's topic?

But when I went back to re-read my half-written draft, I realized this was my essay's topic. That image of my mother leaning into the forbidding hole and fishing around for the cat walked me straight into the heart of that piece—a meditation on love, loss, and family origin stories, especially those about animals.

Once again, I was reminded to trust the writing process.

A note about focused freewriting: Focused freewrites are often made easier with the use of sentence prompts such as "I remember," especially when you hit a blank wall as you're writing and can't think of anything to say. When that happens, simply write the prompt over and over until some other thought or image comes to mind. Sentence prompts help us keep writing when we have run out of things to say.

For instance, I'm writing this now while seated at a study table on the second floor of a university library. I write here a lot, finding the atmosphere both comfortable and inspiring. If I wanted to bring up images of all the different places I've written in over the years—coffeehouses, libraries, the subway, even my own house, I might try a freewrite using the focus "Where I Write," and the sentence prompt "I write in…." I'd be in search of specific details about those places. The sentence prompt gets me started and, more important, keeps me going when I get stuck.

And though you may begin a freewrite with a particular focus, some totally unrelated memory or image may come up. If it feels like there is a real pull to go there, then do so. The most important thing is to use these techniques to help you unearth and write your way into the good stuff. To do that, you must follow the writing wherever it leads you, even if that ends up far away from where you started.

3. Description

The basic elements of our stories—setting, characters, and action—all require description. I find in my own writing—and that of my students'—that this is often the most challenging part of storytelling.

A good strategy when describing the memorable people, places, and events in our lives is to stay grounded in our senses. What do we remember seeing, hearing, smelling, touching, or tasting in any particular experience? What word or words best describe these details? For starters, we can never go wrong using proper nouns; they let us know we live in a real world of specific people, places, and things: it was a 1958 red Chevy, not a car; they were the McBrides, not the next-door neighbors; she wore Birkenstocks, not sandals.

In addition, our adjectives should be apt, but not overdone, and our verbs should show some action or mood. We can also take advantage of figurative language, including simile, metaphor, and personification: She moved through the room like a cat; his garden was an impressionist painting; the moonlight led him safely through the dark woods.

Paying attention to these elements of description helps us do more showing than telling, the cardinal rule of storytelling.

For instance, rather than simply saying that your whale watching trip was "amazing," think of what would show that: the sound of the whale breaching; the briny smell of the ocean; the slant of the light on the water; the rocking of the boat; and so on. All these sensual details give evidence for your experience of amazement.

Try this descriptive exercise for practice: Go sit for 15-30 minutes in a public place with your writing journal, inside or outside, day or evening. Get comfortable, then open your journal.

Begin with the sentence prompt "I see" and describe in as much detail as you can all that you see in this place. When you feel complete with that sense, move on to the next sense prompt "I hear." Write in the same detail as with the first. Go through the rest of the five senses. As you write, stay focused only on the sense that you are describing. Notice which details seem the most interesting or telling about this place. More important, which of these details communicate your experience of this place?

4. Character Sketch

When you use the character sketch technique, you do more than simply describe someone physically. That's important, of course, as s/he will come more alive on the page the better that you—and your intended reader—can see what that person looks like, sounds like, moves like.

But a character sketch becomes more interesting when you add the person's relevant personality traits and significant biographical information.

For instance, if I were to do a character sketch of one of my favorite high school teachers, I'd include her height (short), athletic skill (she was our phys ed teacher), and coloring (her small, olive-dark face). I'd also mention how young she was, and how demanding she was of us. I'd describe how she looked while bouncing down the school halls (even when not wearing tennis shoes), gesticulating wildly alongside her friend and colleague, a much taller, paler, and mellower teacher. Oh, and I guess I would mention that she was a nun who dressed in the black and white habit of her religious community—both in the gym and out.

I'd include relevant biographical information—a matter of keen interest among her former students, especially her decision to leave the convent after 20 years, marry a much younger man, sail around the world with him for a year, then return home and open a pizza parlor.

As I sit here now and write about the former Sister Joseph, more images of her come to mind, each small detail leading to another, and another, and then finally to a specific scene:

It is 1958 and our girls volleyball team has gathered after class in the school gym for practice. As we fumble our way around the court, Sr. Joe paces up and down the sidelines, barking orders at us, her black veil tied behind her back with a fat rubber band, the dour nun shoes exchanged for bright white tennies. Her diminishing patience at our ineptitude now exhausted, she charges onto the court, to the spike position of my team. She pushes aside Loretta, our best player, and yells "Set me up!" to the quaking server next to her. We all stand there, still as stones, and watch as Sr. Joe rises like some fiery rocket and hammers that ball over the net.

A Final Word About These Techniques and Their Purpose

The writing techniques are meant to guide you to your stories; they are not an end in themselves. You can use each to get started and keep going. Then when you discover an important experience or memory, you can stop using the technique—the list, the freewrite, etc.—and concentrate instead on the story that's waiting to be told.

Those stories are typically written in sequence, as chronologies of particular events or experiences. For instance, if you wanted to record the story of your brother's car accident, you might begin: I got up Wednesday morning. I showered, dressed and had breakfast. I took the 8:04 a.m. train to work for my 9 a.m. client meeting. At 10 a.m. my mother called to tell me my brother had been in a serious car accident and was now in the emergency room. I jumped up from my desk and ran into my boss's office, crying. And so on.

The trick in storytelling is pacing. In the above account, for instance, it isn't necessary to include all the steps in the process leading to the dramatic phone call. So while we can tell our stories chronologically, we need to decide what actions to include, which to omit or condense, what to linger over, and where to speed things up. When our story is well-paced, we build to the climax in a timely fashion.

Several years ago, I was hired to join a neighboring family for a Sunday afternoon walk in a nearby nature preserve, then help each person write about the experience. My small class consisted of a young couple in their late thirties and their three children—10-year-old Michael; 8-year-old Erin; and 5-year-old Henry.

It was a beautiful fall day and, as luck would have it, we spotted a deer not long into our walk, a lovely doe who stood close, though not for long. Urban dwellers, we were all startled and thrilled with this animal encounter, none more so than the children.

Thirty minutes later, when we were all seated at a dilapidated picnic table, I gave instructions for how to write about our walk. After 15 or so minutes of writing, everyone finished, then read their story aloud.

Not surprisingly, all three of the children wrote about seeing the deer. Henry, in his impeccable 5-year-old directness, simply wrote two "true" sentences that Hemingway would admire: "I saw a deer. It was close."

Erin wrote a lovely free verse poem, impressionistic and full of color, capturing the emotion of that special moment. Ten-year-old Michael wrote a fully developed, if brief, narrative, beginning with our arrival at the preserve, the start of the walk, and then building to and ending with the sudden appearance of the deer. He made no mention of the remaining hour of our time there, nor needed to. His rendition was perfectly paced, and sequenced, and led artfully to the dramatic moment.

Was Michael especially gifted at telling a story? Perhaps, but more likely he was demonstrating what we know to be true of human beings: we are hard-wired for narrative. Stories are the primary way we organize and recount our experiences, bringing order to seemingly random events, and discovering their significance in the process.

Chapter 3

TELLING STORIES ABOUT PEOPLE

People are the characters in our lives: the heroes and villains, helpmates and foils, friends and enemies who we act with or react against. Some of our people play major roles, others minor. Some show up early, then may disappear; others may not come on stage until we're well into adulthood. But whenever they arrive, and however long they linger, these people help shape us, for better or worse, and so become a major source of our life stories.

The following exercises and contributor submissions will help you access your stories about people.

Family of Origin

How do we begin to write about our original family—that rich and complex cast of characters who shaped us, who we carry with us, who may haunt us still? One way is to just list them all, especially the major players in our family dramas: our parents, siblings, grandparents, aunts, uncles, cousins—all those family members who had the most significant impact on our developing selves, in both large ways and small, for good and, in some instances, for ill. These should be the people who we spent considerable time with, who showed up regularly in our lives, or who were present at some significant portion thereof.

In my case, the list of those people would be quite small. My parents and one brother. Three people, not counting all the animals who shared our home. Everyone else—surviving grandparents, a meager number of aunts, uncles, and cousins—lived 700 miles away, which, in the '40s and '50s, might as well have been 7,000. But that notable absence of a larger extended family is really a story in itself. And when I use the sentence prompt "What I notice about this list is...", I start to discover that story.

What immediately emerges are certain images and family themes: the annual visits we made to Philadelphia, the place my parents left early in their marriage for Chicago; my relief as a teenager at not having to endure holidays with relatives; my mother's recurring sadness at living so far from her parents, sister, and a much-beloved niece; my almost-obsessive need to stay in close touch with current family members who now live far away from me.

Following are 4 writing prompts to help you tell stories about the family you were born into—or became part of through adoption

For the ***first***, list the major players in your family by name, then use the sentence prompt "What I notice about this list is..." to explore what this list reveals to you about the family you grew up with. Be sure to mention the role specific family members played in your life. Let whatever images or scenes about your family emerge and see what particular stories they lead you to.

And then some: Pick one person on your list, a particularly interesting or colorful family member, one you know a lot about, either directly or indirectly. Then put his or her name at the top of the page, and, using the sentence prompt "I remember," write down all the memories you have about this person. Then record one of them in more detail.

And then some more: Go through your list again and note the family member you most admire. Use the character sketch technique to describe this person physically, while also including important biographical information. Finally, write about why this person is so admirable, giving specific examples from his or her life.

And just one more: Do the above exercise with the person on your list that you feel has been the most troublesome in your life.

From the Trenches

Justine writes about a typical Sunday dinner with her family

On Sunday afternoons we'd go pick up Uncle Stevie, my grandfather's baby brother, from his one room apartment in Hoboken and drive him back to my grandparents' for dinner. He'd spend the afternoon sitting in the straight backed stuffed chair next to the window, a whisky in one hand, a cigar in the other. His shirt buttons stretched across his big round belly.

Uncle Stevie liked to pontificate over dinner. Mouth full, fork held aloft to make a point, he'd speak as an authority on any subject, even though he only finished the 4th grade. He'd goad whomever he could into an argument, smiling and raising his big bushy eyebrows, challenging anyone to debate him on any subject. As a 19-year-old college sophomore, I was usually the target. Normally, standard dinner talk was of the weather, the news, the sale on fruit at the A&P, except for Sundays when Uncle Stevie was invited.

I remember one particular Sunday dinner at my grandmother's. The table was set with the lace tablecloth covered with a sheet of plastic, the house smelled of lasagna and the sound of my cousin raising holy terror echoed off the walls.

At five, my cousin Michael was uncontrollable. He greeted us all that Sunday with a raspberry in the face. He stunk of perfume, because he had just knocked over my grandmother's dressing table. He'd been to the basement once already to play with the thermostat and unplug whatever he could. My aunt's response to all of this was a tired, "Michael."

Once my grandmother had set the food out, the dinner table was as colorful as a Christmas tree. "Dinner," she yelled. We made our way to the table and sat down. It was quiet, pleasantly so. Then we realized Michael had wandered outside to the yard. It was a summer afternoon and the door to the dining room was open. We could all see him clearly, so without concern we started dinner. "Salute," we toasted and then started filling our plates.

Talk of the sale on fruit at the A&P ensued. Just as Uncle Stevie lifted his fork to comment on something other than discounted produce, we got hit full force with a stream of cold water. We turned to see Michael in the doorway, grinning and gripping the garden hose, shooting water across the table, gleefully aiming at each of us in turn.

We all sat, stunned and soaked. Then Uncle Stevie jumped up from his seat and yelled, "Why doesn't somebody smack that kid?"

Silence. I stared down at my plate, at the lettuce swimming in a puddle of water. Finally someone had said it, said what we'd all been thinking every Sunday for the last two years.

My grandfather broke the silence. "Stevie, why do you always have to open your goddamned mouth!"

We all got up to dry off what was left of dinner. Michael went back outside to play and we finished the meal talking about the weather and the sale on fruit at the A&P.

Current Family

My own current family reflects both my marital and parental status—divorced and childless—as well as my age; with the recent death of my father (at the amazing age of 95), both of my parents are now gone.

My lone generational peers, excluding distant cousins, are an older brother and his first wife Pat, the mother of two of my nieces and an important part of my current family life. (My brother's second wife died.) This down-sized version of a family may be familiar to some, one defined as much by absence as by who remains.

And who chiefly remains for me are three grown nieces and a nephew, their spouses and children. And while I have many wonderful stories to tell about these "kids" (the oldest is now 44), my most compelling family stories are about how things got this way—all those deaths, marriages, divorces, and re-marriages, all the fallings out and reconciliations.

There is lots of drama in these stories, enough to fill many hours of writing.

Following are 3 writing prompts to help you tell stories about your current family

For the ***first,*** list those people who are presently a part of your family. Include spouses, partners, significant others, children and grandchildren, nieces and nephews, parents and grandparents, siblings, and of course the in-laws.

Now list those adjectives that describe your current family. "Fractured" is one I've used when referring to mine, which is less a judgment than a description. Other adjectives are on the sunnier side, including "talented," "generous," and "fun."

Take one of your adjectives and use the freewriting technique to bring up all the images and scenes that exemplify that adjective. In the process, see what particular stories emerge.

And then some: Go down the list of your family members and choose two or three who represent your most conflicted relationships. Pick one and describe the nature of that relationship, including incidents that illustrate the trouble between you. See if in the writing you begin to better understand this relationship.

And then some more: Select the person from your list whom you wildly love. Then use the character sketch technique to describe this person, making sure to include all of those characteristics and traits you especially hold dear. See if in this exercise you are led to a particular story about this person, especially one that illustrates why you are so crazy about him or her. Tell that story.

Mothers & Daughters; Fathers & Sons

In one of my recent writing workshops, many people wrote of their enduring relationship with the same-sex parent or child: there was the grieving daughter who'd recently lost her mother; a mother and her on-going struggles with an adolescent daughter; and the son still unable to forgive his father.

These are classic stories, reaching back into antiquity and deep into our psyches. They are universal stories; each of us has been a mother or a daughter, a father or a son. And each of us has experienced some conflict in that relationship. It's inevitable and it's dramatic. And so the stories we tell about this bond are inherently rich and complex.

My own mother-daughter stories would include:

- the day my mother took me to buy my first bra;
- the summer nights we'd stay up 'til 3 a.m., just the two of us, playing cards and eating cold fried chicken;
- the one and only time she slapped me, when I was 15 and talked back to her;
- and standing in the bathroom of our house on East End Avenue, helping my mother change the bandages from her recent mastectomy.

Following are 4 writing prompts to help you tell your mother-daughter/father-son stories

For the ***first***, make a list of all the images you can bring up about your same-sex parent. Go as far back in time as you can remember. Get specific and let one image lead you to another. Then choose one entry on the list and describe it in more detail. Then do this ***same exercise*** with your same-sex child.

And then some: Make a list of images that come up for you about you and your opposite-sex parent. Think about the rosy, loving times as well as the not-so-rosy and loving. Get specific when listing these images, then stop when one leads you to a particular memory you want to record in more detail. Then do this ***same exercise*** with your opposite-sex child.

From the Trenches

Dave writes about a terrifying experience with his father

When I was five years old, I lived next door to Melvie. If I wanted to play, I went over to his back steps and hollered, "MEL-vie." If he wanted to play, Melvie would come up on our front porch and look in our front window, cupping his hands around his eyes to see what was going on inside.

One evening after a disrupted supper, my father, who was an alcoholic and "off the wagon" at that time, was ranting about something in his life that was going very wrong. That could have been anything.

He was stomping around in his big 4-buckle overshoes and black mackinaw, yelling at my mom and shooting me murderous glances.

I was glad when I looked out the front window and saw Melvie on the porch. Maybe I could escape the trouble. I asked my mom, "Can I go over to Melvie's?"

My dad acted before anyone could say anything. He took three great, angry strides toward the front of the room, raised his right overshoe, and kicked the window into bits, inches from Melvie's face.

Melvie may not have believed what he was seeing, so he stayed in place, hands cupped over his eyes, while the glass splintered and crashed in front of him. A window screen was all that saved my friend from God knows what—serious injury, sliced jugulars, disfigurement. He turned around and went home.

Before I saw him again days later, he had no doubt told and retold the story. We didn't talk about it. I was pretty ashamed.

Over time, Melvie and I, living in different cities, only saw each other every decade or so. I wondered sometimes if he carried that image into adulthood as I did. My question was answered fifty years after the fact when, in one of our reunions, he casually asked me, "Do you remember that time your dad kicked the window out?" He wouldn't say whether the question was a nostalgic recollection or the attempt to cleanse a persistent and primal terror.

Sib Stories

Of all our family relationships, none survive longer than those with our siblings. Typically, we clock in more years with our brothers and sisters than with our parents, our spouses, or our children. More than sheer length, though, our relationship with our sibs is unique in how deeply it connects us to our family of origin, to the host of memories we have growing up in that family, and to our own self-identity.

For all that, this singular relationship is both under-appreciated and often misunderstood. We may even minimize the impact our sibling relationships have on us. I think of my friend Rose, one of siblings, whose closest sister Naomi became tragically disabled in her early twenties. Sympathy poured in for Naomi, of course, and for her parents, but little attention was paid to Rose and her feelings. Few people, Rose included, recognized the depth of her loss and how she was changed by it.

Following are 3 writing prompts to help you tell your sib stories

For the ***first***, list your brothers and sisters by name. Then choose the sib that you felt closest to growing up, and use the character sketch to describe him or her. Start with a physical description—how s/he looked, spoke, moved—and then let that lead you to some specific images of the two of you together. See if one of those images leads to a particular story worth recording.

And then some: Do the same exercise with the sib you felt most conflicted about.

And then some more: Our sibling allegiances often change either while we're young and/or as we grow into adulthood. If that has happened to you, describe when and how that happened. Be sure to use specific incidents or experiences to illustrate that change.

From the Trenches

Pat writes about her closest sib, Gloria

For most of my childhood, I was the baby of the family. My sister, Gloria, was three and my sister, Mary Lou, was seven when I was born. To everyone's surprise, my little brother, Paul, came along when I was 12. In the early years, Gloria and I did everything together. We were playmates, confidantes, partners in crime. My mom bought us the same toys, dolls, cutouts, and games. It was as if we were twins, though given our age difference, I was amazed that Gloria would do what I asked—without question or hesitation.

My present for my fifth birthday was a trip to the circus. My father bought the tickets six months in advance and my mom made a calendar to count off the days. The big day came and it was everything I had hoped for and more. What I loved the most were the beautiful ladies in sequined, gauzy costumes standing on the backs of white horses riding around one of the rings in the three-ring circus. It was magical.

On a Saturday afternoon, several weeks after the circus, Gloria and I were riding our tricycles in the back yard. It was a lovely summer day. Our tricycles were bright red. Gloria's was larger than mine by about a foot and a half. I had a brilliant idea. If she would just stand on the seat of her trike and hold her arms out, I would push it. She'd be just like the beautiful ladies on horseback in the circus.

She climbed on the seat, stood up, and held her arms out. I pushed the tricycle, and—I can still see it in slow motion—she promptly fell head first, over the handlebars, to the concrete sidewalk, onto her nose. She just lie there, blood everywhere.

I ran up the three flights to our apartment screaming all the way. My father flew down the stairs. Much of what followed is a blur, but I remember the trail of blood from the backyard up the stairs and through the apartment.

Then there was the first time we went riding in Dad's brand new 1948 Packard, the first new car he'd had and he was so proud of it. The back seat had a built-in cigar lighter. This was something new. I pushed it in, waited it for it to pop out, and handed it to Gloria. "Put it on your nose to see if it's hot." I said. She did. And it was. That kid had a blister the size of a walnut on her beezer for days.

I remember the week's vacation to Camp Lake with the family. Lots of kids, games, swimming, gym sets—and a trapeze. "Gloria," I said, "while you're on that trapeze, why don't you fall back and hang by your legs like the ladies in the circus. I know you can do it. It will be so beautiful." She fell on her head and was in bed all day.

During our teen years, there were many more instances of Gloria following my "suggestions" and "advice." For instance, when she was a freshman in high school, I told her we should learn how to smoke, that she'd looked cool if she smoked. We learned together, and she did look cool.

When she lay dying of cancer eight years ago, she told me, "I'm not going to die. My little sister said so." Dear God, I wish that just that one time I could have been right.

THE KIDS IN OUR LIFE

When my great-niece Nell was two years old, we started hanging out together: regular trips to the park, to bookstores, and, of course, the local muffin shop. And one day, we wandered into a pet store. It was located just down the street from a children's bookstore, where we'd spent a good part of the morning reading picture books and hugging stuffed animals.

It was a dark and crowded little pet store filled with frogs and turtles in glass tanks, brightly colored birds in big cages, and one resident kid-averse cat, big and dull gray, who ran and hid soon after we entered. We were only there a short time (you're only anywhere a short time with a two-year-old), but it was such a memorable experience that I entered it in my journal later that day. Here is an excerpt:

"We arrived at the pet store and immediately saw Little Dude, the owner's child-wary cat. Still we managed to sneak in a couple of pats before he bolted. Then we headed down one of the crowded aisles to the aquariums full of frogs and fish and iguanas, the last of which Nellie pressed her little face against and kissed.

"But it was the birds she really liked. All puffed up and feathery, at least 30 of them were pacing back and forth in their large cages, chattering loudly.

"As we approached them, I picked Nell up for a better look. She was riveted, eyes wide and staring. Then she stuck her arms wide out in mid-air, turned to me and asked, 'But what are they saying??' Then repeated the question again and again, each time her little arms outstretched and bouncing, a mix of frustration and amusement in her voice."

Use the following ***writing prompt*** to re-live one of your special kid moments. These can be your own children or grandchildren, nieces and nephews, or the children of friends and neighbors.

Begin with a list of their names, then select just one and start writing down as many images or scenes as you can remember of time spent with this child. When one of those scenes comes into sharper focus, stop and more fully describe the entire experience. If you recall any dialogue in this story, especially that of the child, or between you and the child, weave that into your account.

Over time, keep moving down your kid list—and keep adding to it. If you're lucky, you will never run out of stories to tell about the kids in your life.

People from Grade School

I recently had a phone chat with my great-niece, Nell. She's now in 4th grade and is having girlfriend troubles. It's the tribal thing, of course—who is and who isn't part of the tribe, who gets admitted, what the entry requirements are, who gets tossed. This is very serious stuff and Nell's concerns are heartfelt. As I listen, wanting to be helpful, I suddenly see my own 9-year-old self at St. Domitilla's grade school in suburban Chicago, trying to navigate some equally troubled waters.

It's morning recess and I've just sidled up to the cool girls standing in a loose circle on the playground. The loud and giddy talk ranges from clothes to boys to the teachers we love to hate. I'm new to the school, shy, chubby, and dressed funny. As the conversation becomes more animated, punctuated with laughter, some of it mean, aimed mostly at the girls in the out-group (me?), the circle slowly begins to close. I stand there helpless as the girls on either side of me move in and lightly touch shoulders, leaving me standing alone on the outside. The sound of those doors slamming still echoes in my ears.

Following are 3 writing prompts to help you tell some of your grade school stories

For the ***first,*** head a list titled "Friends & Foes" and begin to write down random images of your grade school classmates. Don't worry if you can't remember names or specific details.

Just list particular scenes as they come up—in a classroom, on the playground, on the school bus, at a school dance—and when one of these exerts a particular pull on you, start to describe that scene as well as you remember it. See where it leads you.

And then some: Make a list of the teachers, counselors, and coaches from your grade school experience. If you can't remember names, identify them by some physical characteristic ("the 4th grade teacher we called 'piano legs'"). Then select one from the list and start to describe this person in some detail. See if any particular memories emerge.

And then some more: In 5th grade, I had a mad crush on Jerry H., a cute freckly-faced boy shier than I was. I doubt we ever spoke more than 50 words to each other—and most of those were during school outings, where we were safely surrounded by hordes of classmates and teachers.

Still, I yearned for more of a connection. The most vivid memory I have from this time is of walking up and down the street where he lived with his parents and older brother, in one of those uninteresting ranch houses so prominent in the '50s suburbs. One day, after weeks of this, I snuck up to the rear of the house and snatched a flower from a blooming lilac bush. Triumphant, I ran home and pressed it into my scrapbook, thrilled that I now possessed something that belonged to my true love.

Use the freewriting technique with the focus "Grade School Crushes," and see what interesting images or stories you unearth from this tender time in your own romantic youth.

From the Trenches

George writes about a grade school kiss that had a lasting impact

I remember my first real kiss. It wasn't one of those smooches with Mom or my cousins Basia or Teresa, but an honest-to-goodness kiss, in the third grade at Henry D. Lloyd grammar school, at the ripe age of eight, with Leslie. Leslie was good looking, even then: long straw-colored hair, sometimes worn wrap-around crown style, light blue eyes, and a gleaming smile.

The kiss happened on a fine spring day in 1962, during recess, between 10:25 and 10:45 a.m., birds and bees style. We were on the school playground, which was divided in half by a long white line, separating the girls' from the boys' side. As the girls' water fountain wasn't working that day, Leslie, thirsty, crossed that white line and was now in boys' territory. Something moved me to think that this was more than the mere crossing of a geographical line.

Coincidentally I was also thirsty, and so headed to the same fountain. And although I was on my side of the line, my brain told me I was also crossing a border with Leslie.

After Leslie took her drink, I moved forward to take mine. But Leslie blocked the fountain, saying, "Kiss me."

"You want me to kiss you?" I countered, amazed.

"Yes," she replied, and set in motion images of Humphrey Bogart and Ingrid Bergman in Casablanca, and Errol Flynn and Olivia DeHaviland in Sherwood Forest. Now here were Leslie and George in front of hundreds on the playground at Shakespeare Avenue and Lamon Street in Chicago. Sweeter than Mom's home-baked paczki or bismarks, Leslie's parted lips were moist, warm, and tender.

A buzz erupted and, like the hum of bees, spread across the playground. But this was a different buzz than the one that signaled the end of our recess. Upon settling into our classroom seats, Deborah blurted out to our teacher, "Miss Hackert, George and Leslie kissed at recess." I saw a brief smile cross Mrs. Hackert's face right before she led me out of the classroom for a private conversation.

People from High School

High school is a critical time for most of us, so it is no wonder that many of our important, even dramatic, stories originate there: stories of classmates, best friends, and hated enemies; of dances, sports events, and talent shows; coming-of-age stories about first loves, finding our place among peers, finding even our life's work. For some there are dark stories as well, of troubles at home or at school. And of course there are stories about the adults from that time: those teachers, coaches, and counselors who inspired us, saved us, or whom we barely survived.

In my writing workshops, I regularly invoke the spirit of my freshman English teacher, Miss Pirman. I'd arrived in her class ill prepared in the basics of English grammar and so she'd volunteered to tutor me on her own time after school, to help me catch up with the others. I can still see us sitting there in that empty classroom, the thin autumn light coming through the windows, me hunched over at my desk, her next to me, that quiet, encouraging voice leading me through the monotonous grammar drills.

It was in that tedious process that Miss Pirman unwittingly instilled in me an enduring love of words, which she then recognized by publishing my first poem in our class anthology. It was a bouncy little paen to a St. Bernard dog that I can recite to this day.

Following are 4 writing prompts to help you tell your stories about people from high school

For the ***first,*** list the memorable teachers, coaches, and counselors from your high school experience. Make the list as complete as you can. Then circle your most and least favorite from the list, and for each one do the following exercise.

First just describe him or her physically—what do you recall he looked like, dressed like, sounded and moved like? Did she have any distinguishing physical characteristics or mannerisms? Then describe what each did at your school and what your relationship was with him or her.

After you get that basic information down, start to write—in no particular order and as fast as you can—as many images and scenes about the person as you can remember. See him or her in your memory—in the classroom or the hall, on the ball field or in shop class. Write down all of the different random memories you have about this person and then when a particular experience comes up in the writing—a specific encounter or event—go on to tell that story.

And then some: Do this same exercise for bringing up memories of your best friend and worst enemy from high school.

And then some more: Use the focus phrase "High School" and the sentence prompt "I remember" to do a 10-minute freewrite exercise. Begin writing in any random order all the scenes, images and details you remember from your high school experience. If you get stuck at any point, write the prompt over and over until memories start to come again. When one specific experience or event comes up in the writing, go on to tell that story.

And then just one more: Using the monologue technique, have a conversation in writing with your favorite high school teacher, coach, or counselor ("Dear Miss Pirman"). Tell him or her why s/he was your favorite. Get specific.

From the Trenches

Pat writes about her teacher from high school

Sister Vitalis? What a funny name we twittering 13-year-olds thought starting high school at an all-girls Catholic school in Chicago. All we could think of was the men's hair cream, which of course made us giggle even more. Sister was under five feet tall and probably weighed less than 80 lbs. soaking wet. She taught English and you better be darn sure that you knew how to diagram sentences no matter how complex they might be, and how to speak correctly and clearly. (To this day, whenever I have to write something, I'm glad that Sr. Vitalis isn't grading me on it.)

One of my very favorite memories of her is when we were sophomores and got to go to the Father-Daughter Dance. It was really a big deal to me. I think it was the first time my Dad and I ever did anything with just the two of us, without my brothers or Mom. It was a special night, he wore a suit and tie and I was in heels. As we arrived at the school, the nuns were all lined up to greet the girls and their dads. Well, my Dad took one look at Sr. Vitalis and burst out laughing. Turns out she had taught him in the second grade, her very first year of teaching. She must have been in her early 20's then and my Dad told her how all the little boys in the class had a crush on her. Sister laughed and laughed. From then on, Sister would ask every so often how my Dad was doing, and it made a special bond for all three of us.

When Sr. Vitalis retired from teaching in

1989, at 84, she formed our high school alumnae association and has served as its moderator since then—having just celebrated her 100th birthday! She asked me at an association luncheon a couple of years ago about my Dad. It seems she never forgot that he had a "crush on her." He had just recently died and having her ask about him was a very special moment for me.

People from College

When I returned to finish my bachelor's degree in 1969, I switched my major to psychology and found myself, much to my terror, in a required statistics course. For each session of that 10 week torture, I sat in stunned silence, staring intently at the board as the instructor produced, at maddening speed, the mysterious mathematical symbols that refused to penetrate my brain.

Much about that class from nearly 40 years ago persists in my memory due to the alliterative name we gave to our esteemed professor, Dr. Dominowski. Because of his outsized balletic movements while at the board, or as he traipsed about the small dingy classroom, we dubbed him the Dancing Dynamo, a play not only on his name and enthusiasm, but on the dizzying effect he had on most of his rapt if uncomprehending students.

I landed on the Dancing Dynamo's name when listing those people I recalled from my undergraduate days. And once I named him, I clearly saw him, dancing in front of that chalk-filled blackboard. I also saw myself, sitting there in the first row, utter confusion playing across my face.

Following are 2 writing prompts to help you recall those people from your college years

For the ***first***, list all the people you remember from your time at college—whether it was just one semester or six years. Then pick one from that list, put his or her name (or brief description) at the top of the page, and describe this person physically. And make sure to place him/her in a specific context. Is this an instructor? A student in one of your classes? Someone you knew from a club or organization? As you write, see what different memories come up. Then go on to describe one of them in more detail.

And then some: Another memory from this time in my life had to do with what was going on at the time outside of that classroom. It was 1970 and the clamor to end the Vietnam war was at full volume. In the midst of it all, four students were gunned down and killed during an anti-war demonstration at Kent State University in Ohio. I recall the agonizing pull I felt. Part of me wanted to leave my studies at the University of Illinois in Chicago and go stand in solidarity with those opposed to the war. The other part wanted to stay put with my head buried in a statistics book, wanting only to finish this course and finally graduate.

Open up the lens from your own college days and see if you can discover any significant political, social, or cultural events that were part of your life during that time. Write about one of them, especially one that created some conflict in you.

From the Trenches

Carrie writes about Greg and how he earned his place among her group of college friends

Greg was filler in our circle of friends—that is until he captured our attention with his new apartment. It was a perk of the job he started the summer before our senior year: the on-call, overnight/weekend body collector for an undertaker in town. In addition to a modest salary, Greg's job netted him an efficiency apartment on the 3rd floor of the funeral home. You got to his apartment either by going through the embalming room and up the back stairs or through the front parlors where the wakes were held. He shared the adventures this job brought into his life, including the story of the poor "stiff" who had to be strapped to the stretcher to be removed from his attic home. Greg lost his balance and the corpse cart-wheeled down the remaining stairs!

Greg was to limit visitors to his apartment and keep the gatherings dignified. And while he mostly succeeded, it was hard to resist the pull of Halloween night and the chance to party at the funeral home. The place sat on the side of a hill with narrow, steep steps leading from the street to the front door. It was gaunt looking and precariously close to the street, as were many of the houses in this old river town. Inside, it was clear that six people made Greg's place crowded, and by the time 25 had arrived, the party had to relocate to the large main parlor. Bless the poor soul who was awaiting goodbyes from his family in the morning. Tonight, he was the recipient of our modified game of spin the bottle: the irreverent Halloween rules established that we were to kiss the man lying in state instead of each other.

The major fright of the evening occurred in the embalming room. That was the entry used so as to not draw attention to the party. We saw two respectfully draped, embalmed bodies there as we hurried through the cold to the apartment. But when it was announced that a jumpy friend (O'Neil) would be coming late, it was decided that he needed a special welcome. Petty, with his porcelain white, size 13 feet, would greet O'Neil from the currently vacant table. He'd lie, covered, with only his feet exposed, then sit upright and groan deeply once O'Neil arrived. The effect was dazzling—both in the terror and hilarity that resulted.

That was 1969, and for us college seniors, Viet Nam loomed. Some had already been called up for physicals and were leaving soon. Wedding plans were fluid. Best to wait two years so as not to end up a young widow. That night we surrendered to the crackling electricity of spontaneity. Though I'm a bit embarrassed to own this folly today, it reminds me of a time when I was willing to play furiously, live exuberantly. I'm glad I had a chance for that dance.

Stories About Romance

My stories about romance seem inextricably wedded to the times in which I grew to adulthood: the tumultuous '60s. So much was going on then—the Vietnam War, the Women's Movement, the fight for civil rights. The war heightened our urgency about romantic matters, and the women's movement changed the way we approached them.

So while men and women still met each other in the usual ways—at college mixers, in bars and clubs, at the endless smoky parties—the old rules no longer held. If I wanted to call Eddie instead of waiting for him to call me, I did (much to his mother's chagrin). If I offered to pick up my date Dieter in my car because he didn't own one, what harm was there in that? (Plenty, according to my father). And if I eagerly agreed to fly to San Francisco to meet Philip on his return from Viet Nam, who would insist I do otherwise? (Well, my father could have, but, in this instance, he knew I wouldn't be stopped.)

Following are 4 writing prompts to help you write your romance stories

For the ***first***, begin with a list of your early romances, those of your late teens and early twenties. These can be both minor and major romances; all that matters is that you remember names and faces. After you make this list, write in random order any scenes and images you recall about these romances. When you hit upon a particularly interesting incident or story, record it in more detail.

And then some: For many people, their most important romances may occur at mid-life, following a divorce, death of a spouse, or a long singlehood. If this is your story, describe how you met your mid-life romance. If this is the story of someone dear to you—a friend or family member—then tell that one.

And then some more: Many of our romance stories involve the one that got away—or the one we sent away, and then came to regret. Tell that sad romance story. And be as forthcoming and truthful about this loss as you can be. See what you discover about yourself in the process.

And then just one more: If you and your main romance have successfully weathered many years together, describe some of the best and worst moments of this long and enduring relationship. Begin with two lists, "The Best of Times" and "The Worst of Times." Then fill in each list with those moments that exemplify each. Now choose one entry from each list and describe it in more detail. When and where did these experiences take place? Who was involved? What happened? As you write, think about what these particular stories illuminate about your long and enduring relationship.

From the Trenches

Janine writes about a significant romance in her life

We stood in the January dark, leaning against our respective cars, looking into each others' eyes. We said little; the attraction was obvious. Over the next few months, we exchanged letters and cards. Seeing mail with a Kansas City return address made my heart skip a beat in an otherwise sad and stressful period of my life.

I was in the midst of leaving my husband, having finally admitted to myself and him that I was a lesbian. I'd told him just months earlier, after we'd been married for a year, but we dragged on for six more months, seeing a therapist, trying to figure out how to tell our family and friends. He was intermittently angry and compassionate.

Hearing from her gave me hope for a life beyond my immediate misery. I knew few other lesbians at the time and so I'd sit at work, a haven from my home life, and write her long letters, pouring out my heart. I told her about the time I went to my local feminist bookstore to buy a book of coming out stories. Suddenly feeling everyone's eyes on me, I picked up a Zora Neale Hurston novel as well, thinking no one would notice the first if I bought both books.

I next saw her six months later, not long after I left my husband. For a few of those July evenings, we were caught up in a new way of loving for both of us. Our kisses were sweet and our bodies tentative. She trusted me, giving me the gift of being her first. And she was my first since officially coming out.

My previous lesbian relationships had been fraught with secrecy and deceit. There was the affair I'd had while married; she told my husband about us during the last week he and I lived together. He ripped up the painting she'd made us as a wedding gift. I was not proud. But, now, for the first time, I was free to love a woman.

I saw her twice more, the last time knowing it would be our last time together. The long distance was too hard and, besides, I'd fallen for someone else. But I will always be grateful for her, always indebted. Wherever she is, I hope she is happy.

Friends: Past & Present

I was born a rambler, spending each summer morning of my childhood exploring the woods, ponds, and fields near my small suburban home. And always at my side were my friends, Butchie and Cosmo, as eager as I to discover the scary spiders and sun-loving turtles along the way. I had girlfriends, too, to play dress up and dolls with, though those early memories seem dimmer.

It was as a teenager, at the all-girls high school I attended, that I really learned about friendship. Without boys to distract us, we girls formed deep and enduring alliances in the classroom, on sports teams, and in school clubs. We learned to be competitive while respectful, supporting and exhorting each other to do our very best, whether in history class, at a school play, or on the volleyball court.

Some 40 years later, I still count many of these "girls" among my dearest friends. Without them, and those other friends I've made over the years, both men and women, my life would be immeasurably poorer.

Following are 4 writing prompts to help you write about your friendships

For the ***first,*** begin with three separate lists: Childhood Friends; Teenage Friends; Adult Friends. Then take some time to fill in each one. Include on your lists both the good and bad friends, those you lost and those you kept, those who enriched your life and those who were, in hindsight, not very good for you.

Now pick one person from each list and, using the character sketch, describe him or her. Remember to include in this description not only what the person looked, sounded or moved like, but also some biographical information and prominent personality traits. As you're describing him or her, see if any particular memories come to mind that you'd like to record in more detail.

And then some: Tell a story about a friendship that was strong at first, but in the end didn't survive. See if you can discover why this particular friendship broke down. You might try writing this story in the third person.

And then some more: Make a list of all the opposite-sex friendships you've had throughout the years. Mine would include not only Butchie and Cosmo, but also Craig, Bob, and Mike, each of whom has contributed to my life in many ways. Work your way down your own list and describe each of these friendships. See what specific images emerge and describe one of them in more detail.

And then just one more: As with a lot of people, many of my important friendships have been tested when one of us moves away, especially far away. Make a list of your faraway friendships that have survived the geographical distances. Then describe in some detail how you've sustained each of these relationships. Pay attention to what particular stories emerge and then tell one of those.

From the Trenches

Muriel's memory of her childhood friend returns whenever it rains

Daughter of an African-American mom and Irish dad, my best friend Janet was blessed with an unblemished "coffee light" complexion, shoulder length dark hair, and dark smiling eyes. If you'd seen Janet when she was 12, you might have mistaken her for the girl on the Girl Scout cookie box. I think frequently of Janet and old times, including our love for dance.

It was a hot rainy day in the city of Boston. Janet and I were aspiring dancers in our mid-teens. According to plan, we met on our way to ballet class, at the corner of Bower and Warren Streets. As we walked up the hill, past the firehouse and the high school, twirling our open umbrellas and sharing our innermost thoughts, thunder and lightning suddenly roared and crackled around us. Torrents of rain began soaking our sandals and turning the sidewalks and gutters into rushing rivers.

We stopped briefly to take off our sandals so they wouldn't be totally ruined. Then, without a word, we both began to sing, "Singing in the rain. Just singing in the rain. What a glorious feeling, I'm happy again!" And as we sang, we danced, imagining we were performing in the movie with Gene Kelly. Before we realized it, we were at the doors of the ballet school. We hurried inside to prepare for class.

Now whenever it storms, as it did on that long-ago summer day, I remember umbrellas, bare feet, singing in the rain, and my friend Janet.

Unconventional People

If you're lucky, you have people in your life who make good copy; their stories are as worthy of telling as your own. Often these are people who have made unconventional life choices, whether in matters of love, career, family, religion, or lifestyle. Some of these choices you might admire, have even facilitated, while others you may disagree with or strongly disapprove of. No matter your opinion of these choices, this is an opportunity for you to tell someone else's story, one with an element of conflict front and center.

I think of my friends Mary and Roy, she white, he black, who married just days before Martin Luther King, Jr. was assassinated in April of 1968. Right after the wedding, they lived with Roy's family, in an all-black neighborhood in Chicago, while waiting for an apartment to open up in a nearby integrated suburb. Mary was literally a prisoner in the house immediately following King's death, Roy fearing for her safety if she stepped outside during the violence that struck the city. While a pretty dramatic result of their unconventional choice, it was neither the first nor the last.

What about those people in your life who've gone against the societal grain? What stories have flowed from their choice?

Following are 3 writing prompts to help you write about the unconventional people in your life

For the ***first,*** make a list of those people in your life who have made unconventional choices, including family, friends, co-workers, and neighbors, past and present, living and dead. Now pick one from this list and tell that person's story. As you do, be aware of what details you include and how you describe his or her unique situation. Add some of this person's pertinent biographical information, then describe his or her choice and its consequences—whether positive, negative, or a combination of both.

And then some: Pick another person from your list and write that story, but this time from his or her own point of view. To help you do that, use the "I" pronoun and write in that person's voice. Try to keep yourself out of this exercise. This will require a leap of imagination and can result in a fun, often surprising writing exercise.

And then some more: Tell the story of an unconventional choice you have made—no matter how long ago or how daring the choice was. You might loosen up your memory by first making a list of those choices, then picking a particular one to write about. Remember to place this story in its context: Where and when is the story's setting, who was involved other than yourself, what happened, and what were the consequences?

From the Trenches

Anne writes about her unconventional aunt—and even more unconventional cousin

Aunt Fran was always a willing outcast. She saw the way her older sister Anne grew up—quiet, polite, never wearing slacks. She saw that a lack of a purpose beyond marriage made Anne doughy and weak, left to find meaning in Hollywood biographies and perfecting the stewed tomato. Fran wanted no part of that life. She wanted one that commanded colorful dresses that swept her knees. She wanted to smoke, especially because it wasn't ladylike.

Aunt Fran likely had more than one boyfriend visit her high-rise studio apartment in downtown Detroit in the'30s. I have a feeling she also made a mean martini and drank alone if the phone didn't ring on a Saturday night.

She had a visible, contagious appetite for life, with no time for fluffy conversations or pointless hair tossing. I've seen pictures of her sitting behind the wheel of a giant Buick, pretending like she knew how to drive. In another one, she's smiling, wearing a long necklace of pooka beads and red and green Christmas bows in her short hair. I picture her in some dark bar, sitting in a red leather booth, drink in one hand, smoke in the other, being completely at ease as the only woman in a sea of laughing men. While other women may have polished silver and waited for 5 o'clock, Aunt Fran would be the Shirley MacLaine of the Motor City Rat Pack.

With this hard-won independence, I can't

imagine how difficult it was for Aunt Fran to tell her mother she was pregnant. At the time, her family had only heard of Don. Fewer had actually met him. Some said he was married. But as usual, Aunt Fran did it her way. She didn't "go away" to have the baby. She became a single mother in the '40s—all but unheard of at the time. She kept the job she loved as a buyer for a large department store, still chain-smoked, and always had a question that demanded more than a 'yes' or a 'no.' She stayed interested and interesting, despite being the one her first-pew Catholic aunties whispered about at family reunions.

Aunt Fran and her sister never spoke of the circumstances surrounding the child named Suzanne. Their slow growing divide became permanent as Anne ran headlong into suburbia and Fran and the baby stayed downtown.

As Suzanne grew, it was clear which parent she resembled. She was popular and had a mind of her own from a very young age. She could get anyone to do anything for no other reason than the way she asked. It was only a matter of time before Suzanne defined her own unconventional lifestyle: she became a nun.

People & Their Stuff

During a holiday visit to the Carolinas, where good friends had recently moved, we were invited to visit their next door neighbor, Mary, a soft spoken Southern lady in her early forties. She was eager to show us her collection of black cat knickknacks, some small and delicate, many life-sized and ornate. And I mean "many." By the time we got to the 2nd floor of her narrow townhouse, I knew this was no ordinary collector.

There were black cats everywhere: on tables, countertops, and bookshelves, placed carefully in cabinets, even crammed onto the top shelves of closets. I tried counting them, but soon lost track. Instead, I just stood there, marveling at our human need to attach ourselves to things—whether one particular object, or, as with Mary, a veritable hoard. (Full disclosure: I am quite fond of my turtle paraphernalia, but I swear I'm keeping it in check.)

Following are 4 writing prompts to help you tell stories of the people in your life and their particular stuff

For the ***first,*** make a list of the family members and friends, co-workers and colleagues presently in your life. These should be people fairly well known to you, people you have some knowledge of and familiarity with.

Now choose one person on the list and begin to make a list of all the stuff you associate with this person. This might include tools, toys, clothing, accessories, knick-knacks, books, and objects associated with sports and hobbies.

After you make the list, choose one particular object you most associate with this person. Put that person's name and the object at the top of the page, such as, "Frank & His Motorcycle." Use the focused freewrite to record all the images of this person with his or her object. Keep writing these random images until an interesting story emerges.

And then some: Do this exercise with someone from the past, maybe someone once close to you who is no longer living—or is simply no longer a part of your life. I think of my mother and her bowling ball or of Phyllis and her ever-present wad of Kleenex.

And then some more: Do this exercise with yourself and one of your own objects as the focus.

And then just one more: Make a list of objects you'd like to be identified with in the future. For instance, maybe you'd like to take up golf, play the guitar, or become a globe-trotting birdwatcher. Whatever the fantasy, do an exercise in which you imagine a story based on you and this object. Suggestion: Though you are invited to make things up in this exercise, try staying within the realm of possibility.

Those Other People

In addition to the major characters in our lives, several minor ones often figure prominently in our stories. I think immediately of Dan, the owner of a convenience store near where I used to live. I would talk to him almost daily when I stopped in for coffee, a donut, or the morning paper. It was the kind of aimless though pleasant chit-chat that cemented our neighborly relationship: conversations about the weather, upcoming travel plans, which stores on the block were opening or closing, all the latest neighborhood gossip.

During one of those amiable encounters, I learned that Dan was a CPA and had once helped people with their income taxes. As a newly self-employed person, I'd outgrown E-Z filing and was confused by all the forms that now replaced it. And so on a particular April 14, still in the midst of doing my taxes, I raced up to the store and had an earnest conversation with Dan in the store's bread aisle. There we huddled as he patiently translated a tax form I was in immediate need of understanding.

Dan is just one of "those other people" who make an appearance in some of the stories I enjoy telling.

Following are 3 writing prompts to help you find your "other people" stories

For the ***first***, make a list of the professionals who've made their way in and out of your life over the years: doctors, dentists, clergy, house painters, plumbers, Realtors, and more—all of those people you've called on for various kinds of professional help. If you can't recall names, just identify them with a couple of words or phrases. Then choose three from your list who make or have made a positive difference in your life. For each one, describe particular incidents or experiences that show how that happened.

And then some: Do the same exercise with three people who've had a negative impact in your life.

And then one more: Neighbors are a special kind of "other people," living just upstairs—or up the street—from where we live or once lived. To discover some of your neighbor stories, use the focused freewrite ("Neighbors") and sentence prompt ("I remember") to see what memories come up. When you come on a particularly interesting neighbor story, tell it in more detail.

SELF-PORTRAIT

One chilly day in November, while strolling through my local cemetery, I noticed an interesting headstone. In addition to the name of the deceased and his dates of birth and death, the following list was carved directly in the center:

Counselor

Teacher

Friend

I don't know if this inscription was the man's idea—or his family's—but I was struck by the importance each role must have had for him. After all, they were cast in stone.

I was also curious to know how he acted in each of these prominent roles: Whom did he counsel and about what? Whom and what did he teach? And exactly what kind of friend was he? What stories, I wondered, lay behind each of these very ordinary but notable roles?

I also thought about which of my own life roles I'd want to appear on such a lasting memorial—ones that someone might walk past and be curious about.

Following are 3 writing prompts to help you write about your own—and others'—important life roles

For the ***first,*** begin with a list of all the roles you've inhabited and currently inhabit in your life, e.g., parent, daughter, brother, spouse, lawyer, beautician, gardener, choir member, artist, college student, and so on. Then choose one — past or present—and write vivid images of yourself in that role. See yourself walking around in this role. Where are you? What are you doing? Whom are you interacting with? Follow yourself around with a mental camcorder and record what you see. Keep writing these images down until you discover one that you'd like to record in more detail. Then, over time, work your way gradually down the list.

And then some: Write about someone else, family or friend, and one of his or her roles. For instance, write about your father as a farmer or your mother as a lawyer. Write about your grandfather as a physician or your favorite aunt as a homemaker and mother. What details come up that show this person living in his or her role? Write those down and see if they lead to a particular story.

And then some more: Imagine your way into a role that you'd like to inhabit some day. Maybe you'd like to be a musician or an Anglican priest or the coach of a Little League team. Maybe you'd like to be a wife or husband, a foster parent or entrepreneur. Write your way into that role by putting yourself into as many imagined scenes as you can. If and when you decide to assume this role, go back and re-read this exercise.

The Life Changers

All of us have people in our lives who have appreciably changed us, especially for the better, and in big ways and small. These people—family, friends, colleagues—may still be in our lives or not, but their influence lingers still.

There is the teacher who saw in us what others did not; the mentor who altered the course of our professional life; the child who opened us to parts of ourselves we thought long dormant. Some of the stories we tell about these people are dramatic, others more mundane.

I think of one culture-vulture friend who introduced me to classical music and foreign films, opening worlds to me I'd never experienced. And of my high school algebra teacher, Sister Katherine, who managed to appreciate both my intelligence and mischief-making. And of that certain boss who, in his orneriness, set me loose to pursue work that really mattered to me. In each instance, these are stories that illustrate the impact these people have had on my life.

Following are 3 writing prompts to help you write about your own life changers

For the ***first,*** use the freewrite technique and the focus "Life Changers" to bring up images and scenes about those people who have positively changed your life. Think about family, romances, friends, teachers, colleagues, even "those other people" who in some important and beneficial way have altered your life. When a particular image leads to a story you want to tell, stop and record it in more detail.

And then some: Often the people who change our lives are those who believe in us—and our dreams—when we ourselves do not. I recall a phone conversation with my eldest niece 15 years ago. I'd begun to waver in my decision to leave a secure job and leap into the entrepreneurial life. In that conversation she gently but persistently reminded me of what I said I wanted—and on more than one occasion. Her willingness to hold onto my truth, even as I was turning from it, had a significant impact in my life.

For this exercise, think of someone who encouraged you to stay true to yourself, even as you may have faltered. Using the character sketch technique, describe him or her and then write about your particular memories of that person. See what particular stories the writing leads you to.

And then some more: Some of our life changer stories resemble before and after photos, showing us our life before this person came along, then after. For instance, I think of how children can enter our lives and change them for the better, especially re-connecting us to family members we've become estranged from.

For this exercise, describe your life before and after someone came along and positively changed it. Who were you before? What mattered to you? What seemed important? Then write about the person who entered your life and the changes that occurred as a result. What was your relationship with this person? Was his or her influence overt or covert? Be as specific as you can, and see what you discover in the process of telling this particular life changer story.

Chapter 4

Place-based Stories

Places, like people, are an endless source of our stories. We are shaped, even changed, by the many places we've inhabited throughout our lives: those places we've lived, worked, and fell in love in; the places we've traveled to or found solace in. When we re-visit these places—near and far, urban, rural or wild, pedestrian or exotic—we find a host of our stories waiting to be told.

The following exercises, and contributor submissions, will help you tell your stories about place.

Places from Childhood: Childhood Home

In a workshop several years ago, I had people write about their childhood home. I did the exercise along with them, and here's one of the images it led me to:

I am standing in a circle in our cramped suburban kitchen along with my parents, some of their friends, my older brother, and two of his friends. It's a Saturday night, during one of my parents' many alcohol-infused parties. I'm 15 or 16 in this particular memory, my brother and his friends just 21. We all have our arms slung loosely around each other, swaying slightly, loudly singing some pop '50s standard—or worse, a sentimental Irish lament.

After trying to take this image and develop it into an essay, I got out of the way and let it form itself into a narrative poem, "Growing up with Drunks," which I later entered into a writing contest. And although I didn't win, I was thrilled to be a finalist. More important, that first poem led to lots of other writing about growing up in an alcoholic home, including journal entries, more poems, and personal essays. And though the material is obviously loaded, telling these stories has been liberating.

Following are 4 writing prompts to help you write about your childhood home

For the ***first***, make a list of the rooms in your childhood home. Next, select one of the more public rooms—the kitchen, living room, den—and use the focused freewrite and sentence prompt "I remember" to bring up as many images and scenes from that room as you can recall. Try not to focus on your thoughts and feelings, but instead write down the details: what you see, hear, smell, taste, and touch in that room. Let these details pile up until you unearth a particular incident or story.

And then some: Pick another of your public rooms and begin to describe the room, again in some detail. Think of shapes, colors, furniture, windows. Notice what memories you recall as you do that and record the most interesting—positive or negative—of them.

And then some more: Use either the freewrite or description technique on any of the more private rooms in your childhood home: your bedroom, your parents' or sibs' bedroom, the bathroom.

And then just one more: Do the freewrite technique and write about any of the outdoor spaces around your childhood home: front or back porch, garden, patio, even the garage.

From the Trenches

Angela recalls an ordinary meal during extraordinary times

"You can call them now," Tante Mathilde says to me. I have been hanging around the kitchen for a long time, watching her stir the soup, put the homemade sausages into it, and, after tasting, add a pinch of salt. Finally! I dash up the steep stairs on hands and feet, open the door to my uncle's tailor shop, and yell "Essen!" Soon everybody will be sitting around the big wooden table: the apprentices, my mother, my two aunts, and my uncle.

I am six years old. It is the middle of World War II. A few weeks ago we were huddled in the air-raid shelter of our house in Berlin. Suddenly a crash and the walls trembled violently. Then we were pushed and pulled through a window. Once outside, we saw that our new house had been bombed into a pile of rubble.

Now Mama, my brother Pete and I are living with my uncle and aunts in the country. This big old house is huge and full of people and cozy places. I run to Tante Liesbeth or Tante Mathilde if Mama says "no" or "don't" to me. Peter has no chance to annoy me; I hide in the tailor shop and play with the scraps of cloth lying on the floor. I daydream in my aunt's bedroom with the silver box full of fancy necklaces on the dresser with the three-way mirror. In the storage room, I find old clothes and a musty smelling fox shawl. I put it around my neck, the fox's mouth biting its tail. I like the way it tickles my nose and makes me sneeze. The old, high wicker baby carriage used by my grandmother for her 10 children is now filled with onions.

No sirens fill our days. I sleep next to my mother under a fluffy cloud of a down comforter. The nights are long and without interruptions.

"I called them," I tell Tante Mathilde, then scoot over to the end of the bench. Right away I hear the two apprentices rush down. They sit with me on the bench. Erich, next to me, tries to tickle me; I must not laugh!

Then we hear the door upstairs open and close. Onkel Klemens descends, the crook of his cane in the vest; it lies on his round stomach like a projectile. He keeps the stiff left leg in front of him, hopping down on his right foot from step to step. Just as Tante Mathilde begins the prayer, "We are waiting for you, oh Lord," he opens the door. With a loud sigh, he sits down. My aunt ladles the soup into his bowl, giving him the largest piece of sausage. Only then is the tureen handed from person to person.

I jab Erich with my elbow; we both try to hide our giggles. The adults talk about enemy planes.

I pray, "Please God, don't let them bomb this house."

Places from Childhood: The Neighborhood

When we're growing up, the small world of our neighborhood seems very large indeed; it includes our house and our friends' houses; the schools we attend; the parks and pools we play in; the places where we worship. In writing about my childhood, I've discovered how much my preference for small, walkable, nature-friendly environments has been influenced by where I grew up.

To stir memories of my childhood neighborhood, I imagine myself in a light plane hovering slightly above it. From this vantage point—this bird's-eye view—I see my house, a modest two-story Georgian; the small backyard and single-car garage; the house next door bursting with all the McGuire children; our main street, Taft Avenue, just a block away with the small grocery and hardware stores. Just to the west are the abandoned railroad tracks; the grade school and church right next to each other; and less than a mile away, the open fields we kids spent long summers wandering through.

The more I can "see" of this place, the more people and events associated with it come into view. Then many of those images lead to stories I want to tell about growing up here.

Following are 3 writing prompts to help you tell stories about the neighborhood you grew up in

For the ***first,*** describe your own neighborhood scene. What do you see from your birds-eye view? Be specific and identify those houses, stores, parks, schools and places of worship that you spent time growing up in. How near or far are these places from each other? What is the natural landscape like? Picture yourself moving around in this neighborhood, and in and out of these places. What particular memories bubble up for you? Pick one of those and describe it in detail.

And then some: Now choose just one of your neighborhood places, and use the focused freewrite and sentence prompt "I remember" to bring up as many scenes and images from this place as you can recall. When you uncover a particular story, record it in more detail.

And then some more: If possible, revisit the neighborhood you grew up in. Walk slowly around and through it, a small notebook or journal in hand. List whatever bits of memory come to you as you go along. Later, tell a story inspired by one of these.

From the Trenches

Liz remembers the neighborhood where she grew up, including one very special dead-end street

In my hometown of Council Bluffs, Iowa, there is a hilly street—Roosevelt Avenue—that dead ends into the side of a bluff. While I was growing up, that bluff functioned as our forest primeval, home to the magical game of "Phantom." Vaguely reminiscent of hide-and-go-seek, Phantom challenged us kids to navigate the slippery hillside slope, searching for a foothold among tangled tree roots, darting among the foliage, then escaping unseen. Breathe at your own peril! In the dusty days of summer, a round of Phantom was the most cherished of events.

Phantom Hill was no ordinary bluff, nor was the five-foot stone wall that held it back. Within that wall was an extraordinary drainpipe, dead center, and round as a hula-hoop. It beckoned neighborhood children with its mystery and challenge. The smallest could squat down or hunch over into the darkness, if they dared—or were dared. How far does it go? How far can you go? I dare you!

Playing ball on that dead end street was the highlight for many Roosevelt Avenue boys—and for me, the only girl, included if there weren't enough boys around to play. When the dead end street was used for our games, the drainpipe became the prime target for batters. It was at the center of centerfield, beyond the manhole that was the pitcher's mound and the pile of stones that served as second base. If your aim was a bull's eye, you were guaranteed a home run. As a bonus you got to watch the outfielder stand and wait for the ball to roll back down the pipe and plop onto the street.

That short stretch of Roosevelt Avenue had many functions. For Kelly, my yellow tabby cat, it truly was a dead end. There she met her maker under the tires of a neighbor's car. But for the Howards, Kretteks, and Caughlans, it was very much alive as baseball diamond, football field, practice range, and launching pad for our lives.

Places of Adolescence: High School

The high school I went to was cobbled together from two very distinct structures: a modern brick classroom building sewn onto an aging convent of wood floors, dark hallways, and worn carpet. When students moved between them—from chapel to gym, or homeroom to geometry—it was like leaving one century and entering another.

It took me awhile to warm to the place, especially since this all-girls Catholic school was not my choice. By sophomore year, however, I was won over. What helped was my experience as a young student athlete. For of all the spaces I inhabited throughout my four years at Nazareth Academy—the classrooms, the auditorium, the cafeteria—it is the gym that holds many of my favorite high school memories. Not only could we be loud and goofy there, but many life-long friendships were forged during hours of basketball practice, volleyball games, even my short-lived cheerleading career.

Then there was that day at the start of our tennis class when I got whacked in the face by my best friend's racquet. I still remember the shock of the blow, my blood dripping on the gym floor, my friend's astonished face, and especially walking around the rest of the day with a sack of melting ice on my face. Fortunately, both my battered nose and the friendship recovered.

Following are 3 writing prompts to help you write about where you went to high school

For the ***first,*** just describe your high school—both from the outside and inside. What does it look like, smell like, sound like there? As you're writing, let specific scenes and images from your time there emerge. When an interesting one comes along, describe it in more detail.

And then some: Now list the different spaces in your high school: particular classrooms, science lab, music room, athletic fields, and so on. Pick one and use the focused freewrite and sentence prompt "I remember" to bring up as many images from that place as you can. See if one of them leads to an event or experience, then write more about it.

And then one more: I didn't play many sports in my first year of high school, but I was a cheerleader. Our squad was coached by one of the lay teachers, though I have only a faint memory of her and our practices. I can more easily recall those nights my father helped me hone my cheerleading skills (he'd been a cheerleader at his all-boys Catholic high school in Philadelphia). I can still see him sitting on the couch in our living room, me standing in front of him waving my festive blue and white pompoms, the two of us in unison shouting out the cheers ("Give us an N, give us an A....")

What memories—good or bad—connect your high school experience with your home life? Make a list of those, then choose one to describe in more detail. Over time, work your way down the list.

Places of Adolescence: Work & Play

Just as I was coming of age in the '50s, the automobile was gaining a foothold in our daily lives. By the time I turned 16, it was considered crucial to own a driver's license and to have regular access to the family car. But my five best friends and I rarely drove out of necessity; it was mostly just for fun. We'd spend warm summer evenings cruising around the adjoining suburbs we each lived in—and with no particular destination in mind. It became one of the major ways we played during this heady time of our youth.

There we'd all be, crammed into one of our parents' modest sedans, the radio at full blast, our laughter piercing the air. And what we seemed to laugh about most was that by the time the evening's designated driver had picked us all up, it was time to turn around and start dropping everyone off.

Following are 3 writing prompts to help you revisit those places you played and worked as a teenager

For the ***first***, start with a list of those places you remember playing as a teenager. In addition to the inside of a 1959 Chevy, my list would include carnivals, skating rinks and swimming pools, neighborhood parks, forest preserves and beaches, and of course pee wee golf. Now use the sentence prompt "I remember" and write whatever images and scenes come to mind. Describe one in more detail.

And then some: Much of our play happened at friends' houses: in basements, backyards and bedrooms—wherever we could secret ourselves away from parents, pesky sisters, and obnoxious brothers. Make a list of your friends from this time in your life and, as you do, see if you recall times you played at their houses. Describe one of those.

And then some more: While in high school, I occasionally "worked" as a babysitter. I've no significant memories from those jobs, likely because most involved my being quietly alone downstairs while the babies slept peacefully upstairs.

But a few of my friends worked real W-2 jobs once they turned 16, most out of necessity. One in particular still resents how that interfered with her high school years. If you worked during your adolescence—full or part-time—write about whether this was a positive or negative experience. Use specific incidents from your job or jobs to illustrate your point of view.

From the Trenches

Mary Ann recalls a memorable night at the town roller rink

I grew up in the '50s, in a town of 4,500 people; this presented a challenge for us teenagers who wanted fun places to hang out. There was Nelson's Movie Theatre, open several evenings a week and Saturday, though the same movie often played for a month. We had the four-lane bowling alley, a popular hamburger and coke shop, the high school gym for dances, and a state park down by the river with caves to explore and streams to wade. Still, there were times when my friends and I had to rack our brains for something interesting to do.

As I was getting ready to enter high school, a skating rink opened up near the highway leading out of town toward Cedar Rapids. The Elms Roller Rink was a big barn-like place with a large wood skating surface, sales counter, coatroom and snack bar. Seventy-five cents would get you an evening of skating and fun, and for another thirty-five cents you could rent a pair of generic red and green shoe skates in something that approximated your shoe size. Eventually, I persuaded my mother that I should have my own skates, pom-pommed to match my skating outfit, which I carried to and from in a white suitcase. The rink was open summer and winter and for several years was the center of our social world, especially on Wednesday and Sunday evenings.

Entering the Elms, we'd see skaters whirling about the rink to taped organ music playing in the background. After changing into our skates, my friend Grace and I would edge onto the hardwood floor like two cars onto a freeway. Merging with the swarm of skaters, we'd secretly glance around to see which boys were on the scene that evening. During the next few hours, a melodic bass voice would announce the various skate sets over the loud speakers.

"Neexxt will be a two-step. Gentlemen, grab your ladies and show us what you've got."

My evening would be complete if Dave O'Toole was there. He was a year ahead of me and I'd had a crush on him since third grade. Usually, when they announced the two-step he would roll up to the side benches where we were seated. Blissfully, I'd skate out toward him until I felt his arm slide around my waist. Then, with my left hand raised in his, we'd skate off side by side, laughing, especially when we'd occasionally trip one another.

On one particular night I turned to see Marty Jo Byers beckon Dave out onto the rink for the Ladies' Choice—the last skate of the evening. The easy smile of anticipation which passed between them as he reached out for her hand told me that something in my world had changed. The lights dimmed further as they pushed off together and the final number of the piped organ music began with the skaters joining in the lyrics: "Goodnight Sweetheart, we-ell, it's time to go...."

"That's it for tonight, skaters. We'll see you at The Elms next Sunday." My heart had been broken for the very first time.

TRANSITION PLACES: FIRST TRAVELS WITHOUT FAMILY

For my high school graduation present, my parents—along with those of my best friends—gave us a week's vacation in Florida. I remember leaving my house the day of our departure, praying I'd make it to the train station without mishap. This was too good to be true: six Catholic girls from the heartland set loose on their own in sunny, sultry Florida.

But, alas, it was the sunny part that did me in. We weren't there a full 48 hours before I was so badly sunburned I couldn't venture forth in daylight for the rest of the trip—at least not without dressing as if I were back in the Midwest on a cold, wintry day.

I did manage to swim in the motel pool, though, at night, and while wearing a dark heavy sweatshirt to protect my raw, blistered shoulders. It was all I could do not to sink to the bottom with the sure wet weight of it.

I only recently returned to Florida, and this time in March.

Following are 3 writing prompts to help you write about your first trip away from home

For the ***first***, list all the highlights of that trip as you recall it, in no particular order. Let that process lead you to some memorable scenes and images, then record one of those in more detail.

And then some: Make a list of the people you encountered on your travels, including fellow travelers, tour guides, and people you met in hotels, restaurants, or campgrounds. Using the character sketch technique, describe one of these people. What did s/he look like? Talk and move like? What do you think was the most interesting aspect of this person? In the writing, see if you can discover why this person still lingers in your memory.

And then some more: What do you think you learned about yourself and about the world as a result of your first solo trip. List the most obvious ("Don't go to Florida in July") as well as the more significant ("What trust our parents must have had in us"). Then write about one of the more surprising lessons on your list, making sure to tell the story that best illustrates that lesson.

From the Trenches

In the context of both the times and the place, Melvin recalls his first trip away from home

At 11 years old, I was already aware of differences among white people and of how they treated Negroes—as we were called then—in different parts of the country. I always felt proud and lucky to be living in Nashville, the capital, and, as we learned growing up, a liberal oasis even in the Volunteer State. I'm sure I already knew even before studying Tennessee history in the seventh grade that my state had been the last to secede from the Union and the first to return to the fold once the war was over. We knew that Nashville was a haven. But East Tennessee—where the third and fourth largest metropolises, Chattanooga and Knoxville, are located—had favored the Union during the Civil War and was the real liberal, civilized, part of the state. I suppose that's why I didn't feel too much trepidation about going on the class trip. We were going east.

That weekend field trip to Lookout Mountain and Great Smoky Mountain National Park was at the start of my seventh-grade year. It was the first time I went outside the city limits by myself. Even though the trip wasn't expensive, my mother couldn't afford it. But I had just started working at the little grocery store up the street, so I was able to pay my own way.

I don't remember what teachers chaperoned us, but vaguely recall visiting some caves. And I especially remember breakfast in Knoxville. In fact, were it not for the grits, I might not remember anything at all. Though I was born and bred in the South, I ate grits for the first time that Saturday morning in Knoxville. I thought it was the best rice I'd ever tasted. I, like most Americans, knew that Southerners were crazy about grits. I had learned that from reading, watching movies and television, and just living. But my family was the exception to the general rule. (Of course, I was an exception to a lot of rules, whether I realized it at the time or not.)

Over 30 years later, when I finally tasted grits again, they were good but not nearly as delicious as those I savored that morning in Knoxville just before turning 12 years old.

Transition Places: First Job

My first job—when I was 20 years old—was in the mailroom of a large regional grocery chain. It was at their executive headquarters, in an outlying suburb of Chicago. Before working there, I'd spent two years at college, wandering all over the curriculum, with no discernible skills to show for it. My father, no longer willing to support my academic confusion, pulled the financial plug, leaving me no choice but to go to work.

The mailroom was on the ground floor of a blocky, two-story gray building. My job was to open the bulky sacks and sort the mail into a big rolling cart, then deliver it each morning and afternoon throughout the building. I'd then collect all outgoing mail, take it back to the mailroom, and run it through the postage meter.

Some days I broke this tedium by working the company switchboard at lunch. Also on the ground floor, it was a small enclosed space off the main entrance, with just enough room for two operators. It was during one of my days on the board, November 22, 1963, that all hell broke loose, the switchboard suddenly jammed. People were frantically calling to tell family and friends that President Kennedy had been shot in Dallas. I remember that particular day, and many that followed, the entire nation filled with uncomprehending shock, horror, and grief. As a result, that otherwise bland and boring place of my first job will forever hold special significance for me.

Following are 4 writing prompts to help you tell stories about the first place you worked

For the ***first,*** simply describe that place. Where and what kind of structure was it? Where was your particular work space? What did you see and hear in this place? Would you describe it as a pleasant or noxious environment? In the process of getting the specific details of this place down on paper, see what particular images and stories begin to emerge.

And then some: Make a list of the people you worked with at your first job. Don't worry if you can't recall names—titles and other brief descriptors will do. Then use the freewrite and sentence prompt "I remember" to bring up as many memories of these people as you can. When an interesting experience emerges, record it in some detail.

And then some more: What was going on in your life during your first job? Put the year or years of this job on top of the page, then list the major moments and events from this time in your life—both personal and cultural. In the process, see if there's any connection between these experiences and the place where you worked. Tell that story.

And then just one more: Another vivid memory from my mail clerk days was a tour they gave new employees of the company's bakery—a large industrial facility next door to the mailroom. It was here that the store's donuts, cakes, and breads were made. During our tour, we talked briefly with one of the bakery staff, a middle-aged woman sitting contentedly on a chair at the end of an assembly line, carefully placing maraschino cherries on each of the cakes that rolled her way. She told us she did this eight hours a day, five days a week, 50 weeks out of every year. That's all I needed to hear. Within three months, I was back in college.

Think of an important decision you made while at the first place you worked, and tell the story behind it.

TRANSITION PLACES: FIRST LOVE

I fell in love with Eddie Meierotto when we were in night school, at Loyola University in downtown Chicago. The campus was located amidst the bars, diners, upscale restaurants, and tony shops along Rush Street, a thriving stretch of hotspots that regularly drew tourists and locals alike. Immediately next door to one of our classroom buildings was a not-so-hotspot, the Interlude, a real neighborhood bar that attracted both evening students and blue-collar regulars.

There was a great juke box right near the entrance—this was blessedly before the ubiquitous sports bars and their blaring TVs—but it never interfered with the conversations we'd have with George the bartender; our fellow students who stopped by after class; or the yellow-haired ladies and red-faced men who called the Interlude home. Nor did it stop Eddie and me from sitting and smooching shamelessly in full view of everyone, our eyes locked only on each other.

I can never think about Eddie without recalling that place so central to our budding romance.

Following are 3 writing prompts to help you recall those places associated with your first love

For the ***first***, describe where and how you met this person, with particular emphasis on how the place itself may have contributed to your first impression of him or her. See if any particular incidents or memories come to mind through this description. Write in more detail about one of those.

And then some: One of the places Eddie and I regularly visited, often with friends, was a small diner in the same neighborhood. A bit on the seamy side, DeMar's was open 24 hours and fed its share of down-and-outers as well as affluent tourists. I can still see us all sitting there—into the late night and early morning—drinking endless cups of coffee, smoking cigarettes, and discussing the finer points of Platonic philosophy.

For this exercise, make a list of those places that you and your first love visited just once, or frequented regularly. Describe one and see what particular memories emerge from the time you spent in this place.

And then some more: List all of the other places associated with this very special person in your life, even if at first they don't seem that special, or nothing obviously eventful happened in them. My own list would include my house, Eddie's house, the places I worked while we were together, and especially where I was when I found out he'd gone missing in action in Vietnam during his second tour of duty.

Make your own list—and stop when a particular story calls out to be told.

Transition Places: First Home

Like many people raised in the '50s and '60s, I didn't move out of my childhood home until I got married. My new husband and I moved into a "garden" apartment in a two-flat on Chicago's near west side, just blocks from a swanky neighboring suburb.

Philip, a Vietnam veteran, and I lived in that apartment for just one year, but what a year it was: Martin Luther King, Jr. and Bobby Kennedy were both assassinated, and President Lyndon Johnson declined to run for reelection.

Still, in spite of these cataclysmic national events, the images that come up for me as I write about our little basement home are all domestic ones, the inevitable settling in of newlyweds to a new place and a new life. One of my favorite images from that life is from the night I overcooked spaghetti for our first dinner party. Philip and I and four of our dearest friends were crammed into the tiny windowless kitchen, no one able to get up once we were all seated. Though I've since learned how to cook pasta, I'll forever savor the memory of that night, of my anxiety and embarrassment, of our friends' forgiving nature, and of my new husband's tender regard.

Following are 4 writing prompts to help you write about your first home

For the ***first,*** write down the street name (and number if you remember it) of your first home and use it as the focus for a freewriting exercise, with the sentence prompt "I remember." Keep writing until you hit on a specific scene or memory that you'd like to record.

And then some: Now describe your first home, both from the outside and inside. What kind of structure was it? What was it made of? How many levels? How many rooms did it have? Where were the windows? And so on. As you go about describing all the details of your first home, see what images come into your mind, then any specific experiences or stories that come to mind.

And then some more: Now do the same exercise for where you lived while in college or the military, in the Peace Corps or as an exchange student.

And then just one more: Make a list of all the national and world events that were going on at the time that you were settling into your first home. Pick one and describe the effect this particular event had on you and your life.

From the Trenches

Shelley writes about an unsettling experience in her first apartment

I remember having a sense of peace in my first apartment. I was content to watch television or write a letter to a friend in this place. But I also felt vulnerable there. One Sunday afternoon, a woman knocked on my door and introduced herself. She told me there had been several break-ins in the building during the workday and that many tenants were calling the management company to demand on-site security. I made my call, voiced my concern, and was politely dismissed. The company did place a security man in the building, however, for a few weeks. Then they gradually cut back on his hours until he was gone completely.

I called my parents and asked them to purchase renter's insurance for me. If I was the next victim, I wanted to be able to replace my few precious possessions. I was worried they would say, "Come home now." Instead, they just added a rider to their insurance policy to cover my apartment. That gave me some comfort.

I tried, too, to figure out ways to protect myself. I believed my unpredictable schedule had shielded me from being taken advantage of so far. At the time, I was working for a domestic violence agency, and if I had to take a woman to court to get an order of protection, I left my place at 8 am. If I didn't have court, I would leave about noon. As an extra precaution, I started leaving my TV on during the day when I left for work.

One day, Shaina, who lived below me, called

to say her place was broken into. I remember picking up the phone and hearing her voice, "The robbers got me." First, she was calm, recounting her day—her door being ajar and calling the police. Then she started cursing and crying. She called the robbers idiots for not taking her Bat Mitzvah jewelry, which was worth much more than the stereo and TV that they did take. I invited her upstairs to talk and drink lots of wine that night.

PLACES FROM ADULTHOOD: HOMES

In September 1994, I went to live in an urban arts residence, in one spare room furnished with discarded motel furniture, shared bathrooms, and communal meals. And best of all—weekly maid service. Located along Chicago's trendy Gold Coast, the Three Arts Club was built in 1912 to house young women studying the visual arts, music, and dance. I was neither young nor, as a writer, representative of the Club's traditional artist-residents. Truth is, I'm not exactly sure why I was there, except for some vague desire to live unencumbered by the demands of daily living; it seemed heaven to be able to concentrate solely on my creative work.

And though I grew to love the daily contact with my fellow artists, I moved out two and a half years later, having tired of dorm living—and of the bird-sized roaches that were as endemic to the place as 3 a.m. gabfests and giggly girls.

But I took with me such wonderful memories of that place, and of the many creative women of all ages, backgrounds, cultures, and artistic pursuits who called the Three Arts home. For these and many other reasons, the Three Arts Club remains one of the most memorable places I've lived as an adult.

Following are 3 writing prompts to help you write about the homes you've lived in as an adult

For the ***first,*** make a list of all those places, no matter how long you lived in each. Now select the home you most enjoyed living in and describe it, with particular emphasis on the specific features that made this home so enjoyable to live in. See if in the process any particular experiences emerge that you want to write about in more detail.

And then some: Now do the same exercise with the home you least enjoyed living in.

And then some more: Pick the home that was the hardest for you to leave. Go back to that place in your imagination, list all of the rooms there, and begin to write your memories from each room. See what stories emerge.

Places from Adulthood: Neighborhoods

When I make a list of the neighborhoods I've lived in as an adult—and these cluster mostly on the north side of Chicago, I'm struck by how walkable they all are. Even when I still owned a car, I'd usually take public transportation, ride my bike, or walk wherever I wanted to go.

This inclination to get places on foot stems in part from having grown up in a small town with a main street just up the block. No one drove us kids to school or the candy store or to visit our pals. We either walked or rode our bikes. And if it was much beyond a mile, we took the bus. Simple, cheap, and healthy.

Throughout my adult years, I've gravitated towards those city neighborhoods that mirrored the one I grew up in, and one especially stands out—Chicago's Lincoln Square. In the seven years I lived there, I easily walked to grocery stores, bookstores, a regional library, three coffeehouses, a couple of pubs, a movie theater and a variety of ethnic restaurants. But best of all, in the midst of all those urban riches, was a community garden with a small, beautifully-restored prairie that bloomed wildly each spring. Many of my neighborhood walks began or ended in that garden. There I would sit quietly on one of the wooden benches and feel a little restored—and wild—myself.

Following are 4 writing prompts to help you write about those neighborhoods you've lived in as an adult

For the ***first,*** describe where you currently live and in some detail. As with some of the other place exercises, start with a bird's-eye view. What's the approximate size of your neighborhood? What other towns and cities is it near? What is the proximity of other houses, stores, schools, natural areas, and other amenities? Be sure to include the features you like and don't like about this neighborhood. In the process, see if there's a particular experience of living there that you'd like to write about.

And then some: Now make a list of all your previous neighborhoods, and choose one of your favorites. List all of the features of this place, including those that made it special. As you do this, see what images play in your mind's eye. Take any of those images and describe it in detail. See what special memories it leads you to.

And then some more: Do the same exercise for your least favorite neighborhood.

And then just one more: Make a list of all the people from one of your favorite neighborhoods, from the corner crossing guard to the next door neighbor to the patrons of your local coffeehouse. Describe your interactions with these people, and when a particularly interesting one emerges, record it in more detail.

Places from Adulthood: Work

Over the years, my work places have included classrooms, retail stores, hospitals, restaurants, and so many bland office spaces they merge into one. As I look over this list, certain images come to mind: the day a student ran to the front of the room and threw up in the waste basket; the morning I finally made it to my office job on time, my boss standing up and applauding; working my first Christmas Eve at a funky indie bookstore, the year the owner brought in several bottles of holiday wine, making an already merry staff even merrier.

One of my favorite workplace stories occurred just days

after I swore off cigarettes. I'd been a dedicated smoker for 20 years, and this was my second attempt. At the time, I was working part-time at a camera store. On Saturdays, people would line up six deep to pick up their photos, frantically waving their little green receipts as the three of us behind the counter searched just as frantically through long bins of envelopes. On this particular day, when I turned to tell an agitated customer that his photos hadn't yet arrived, he whined, "Are you sure? Are you sure they're not there??"

And that's when I snapped, days of nicotine deprivation rising up like some hairy beast, overpowering the good Carol and replacing her with my evil twin. "Just what," I growled, my eyes locked on his, my lips barely moving, "would I have to gain by not giving you your damn photos??"

I felt so much better after that, my withdrawal pangs blessedly relieved. From then on, I highly recommended working retail to anyone trying to quit smoking.

Following are 3 writing prompts to help you tell some of your workplace stories

For the ***first***, list all of your workplaces, then write all of the images that are inspired by this list. In the process, see if a particular story emerges that you want to describe in more detail.

And then some: Now take one of the workplaces on your list and use the focused freewrite and sentence prompt "I remember" to bring up all of the people associated with that place. In the process, see if you recall an interesting event or experience about a particular person. Write about that.

And then one more: Tell a workplace story that's associated with a dramatic event in your life. For instance, just before my boyfriend was to leave for army basic training—and eventually Vietnam—I quit a job I'd started two weeks earlier, wanting to spend as much time with Eddie as possible. I can still see myself sitting in my new boss's office—and the look on his face—when I told him I was leaving. That particular image then leads me to even more memories of me and Eddie, not only from that week, but from throughout that turbulent time in our lives.

Places from Adulthood: Play

For many people, "adult" and "play" don't seem to go together. They work, they take care of their families, they sleep. Aside from TV, the occasional movie, or a baseball game, these people might ask, who has time to play? This is often true for me as well, even though I'm convinced that "all work and no play" can indeed make me dull. So I've figured out one way to make play a more regular part of my life. I schedule one half day each week for a ramble, the goal of which is to wander around and do fun, enjoyable things.

Sometimes I have a ramble destination—a movie, a photo exhibit, a nature hike—and other times I do not. What's important is that I create free open time to move around and let whatever happens happen. This means that if I'm headed for a music event, but find myself veering towards the lake, I take the lake walk, saving music for another day. And if I'd planned on a movie, but suddenly have the urge to go to an art museum, off I go to soak in some culture.

In whatever form it takes, my play begins with a few deliciously empty hours, a walkable city, good shoes, and a willingness to follow any of my (lawful) impulses.

Following are 3 writing prompts to help you revisit your stories about play

For the ***first***, use the list technique to write about how you play as an adult. Head the list, "Where I Play," and jot down those places associated with this part of your life. Think about music venues, sports arenas, museums, theaters, outdoor places—anywhere you go to play. Pick one place from that list, and describe it in some detail. In the process, see what particular memories are associated with this place.

And then some: Many people play best when it's in a structured environment, such as a workshop or class: pottery, art, writing, photography, music, and so on. Make a list of the classes or workshops you've taken over the years to help you play in any of these ways. Then use the focused freewrite and sentence prompt "I remember" to bring up your memories from these various classes. When a particularly interesting one comes to mind, describe it in more detail.

And then some more: A psychologist friend of mine once described sex as "adult play." For this exercise, make a list of places associated with your own experiences of sex as adult play. Then pick one and tell the story associated with that place.

TRAVEL PLACES: NEAR & FAR

When I travel, I tend not to write about my adventures until I'm heading back home. That is, unless something truly memorable happens during the trip and I need to record it immediately.

Usually, though, I just jot down notes in a small notebook throughout my travels, then review them on the plane, train, or bus ride home. I'll make a list of the trip's major highlights—a couple of words or phrases about what seemed most noteworthy. That process inevitably leads to several I want to describe at length.

A recent example followed my travels to the far western shore of Vancouver Island, with my friend Melanie, to the small fishing village of Ucluelet, the correct pronunciation of which I didn't manage until we were long gone.

After making my highlights list on the way home to Chicago, I immediately started writing about our encounter with an adolescent black bear. It happened on the second day of our trip as we made our way across the island to Ucluelet. The bear was just off the shoulder of the two-lane highway, munching his slow way through the tasty flora, unconcerned with the cars that were pulling over so their occupants could gawk at him.

But I was intent on more than gawking. As soon as we came to a stop, I threw open the car door and began to climb out. Somewhere through the fog of my desire to meet and greet this bear, I heard Melanie say, calmly but firmly, "Carol, get back in the car. Get back in the car, Carol."

Following are 3 writing prompts to help you tell some of your more memorable travel stories

For the ***first***, make a list of your travels to far and distant places. When that list is complete, take each destination and do the highlights list. (You will be pleasantly surprised by how much you recall during this exercise.) Then take one of that trip's highlights and write about it in more detail.

And then some: Many of my interesting travels have been within 150 miles of where I live. Not only for the local adventures to be found there, but for the personal discoveries I've made along the way. Do the same exercise above, but with those journeys you've made closer to home.

And then some more: Travel often changes our lives, in big and small ways: we discover a new favorite wine; make a friend; pick up and move to the place that we're visiting. Write about how both your far and nearby travels have changed you over the years. Tell the stories behind some of these changes.

From the Trenches

Paula writes about a faraway place that feels like home

The small medieval town of Bingen sits on bluffs overlooking the Rhine River. Here I wander in a large wooded park, watching the river barges and vineyards in the valley below. Across the river one of the abbeys founded by Hildegard of Bingen is shining a warm gold in the morning haze. From 1098-1179 she lived here, preaching, teaching herbal medicine, writing theology, chant and opera. Hildegard saw divine creativity in the greening of the valley vineyards and the sweet, moist air. Her glorious visions celebrated a sacred cosmos. I am here on a pilgrimage, honoring the 1000th year of her birth.

The air fills with a raucous clanging from the bells of Rochuskapple. Crowds of people gather for an outdoor Mass and festival on this Sunday morning. The chants of the liturgy settle into me as I sit held in the gnarly dark arms of an ancient oak tree. What are my roots in this land? Why do I feel so at home? I don't even speak German. But not knowing the language contains me in a secret, deeper knowing.

Just below the park is a small farmyard where two little girls feed their chickens. One wears a cap like the one I wore at age four. I imagine touching the soft red plush with its tiny embroidered edelweiss flowers. The other girl has long braids to her waist, like my cousin Mia did. The bells start up again, and Mass is over. I get up from my tree-root chair to join the people moving toward the festival stalls. Ahead of me in line stands a sturdy house frau with a long gray braid twisted into a bun. It is my Aunt Catherine's hairstyle. The sight brings me back 50 years to my Aunt's farmhouse kitchen with its unmistakable cozy smells. I watch her make potato salad, enjoying the rhythmic thump of the knife on the cutting board, the tang of a radish slice I pop in my mouth.

A river barge blasts its horn. Now I face a young couple wearing identical bright red shirts. They smile broadly as they sell me a soft pretzel. I take warm, salty bites and watch the faces in the crowd. Some are jolly, beet red and sweaty. Others are somber, drawn into a grim seriousness that reminds me of my father. The bells are still ringing. Every sound and smell and sight is pulling at my heart.

I realize I have lost my glasses and begin retracing my steps back to the oak tree. An older man is sitting there now. He wears a khaki shirt and pants just as my Uncle Leonard did every day. Leonard, a German immigrant to Wisconsin, was a gentle man who loved trees. Nearby are a woman and a little girl sitting together on a log. My Mother, long dead, always wore similar dark dresses and pumps with nylons, even when gardening or walking. The woman and the little girl sit close, hip to hip.

Are my tears for loves I have lost or for ancestors I never knew? Who could I have been if I were born here in Bingen? Might I be a descendant of Hildegard's Benedictine sisters living in that abbey across the Rhine? For over 500 years Hildegard's legacy was repressed but now we are rediscovering her gifts. The abbey is thriving again.

The bells have stopped ringing and an odd

quiet fills me. I continue along the path. Brisk walkers are trying to keep up with their dogs. Two nuns stroll along at a meditative pace. There, just ahead, is the bench where I first sat. Someone has found my glasses. The case is upright, neatly tucked in between the slats of the bench. I smile at the orderliness of the German character. This kind gesture is not a surprise.

From the Trenches

Sharon's travel story is about more than the actual journey

I have been trying to travel to India for the last 10 years, always changing my mind at the eleventh hour. Maybe it was the idea of traveling to India that I loved—breathing in the spirituality of that exotic place.

The first plan was made with two friends, Gary and Robert. We all lived on New York City's east side and would get together once a week to meditate, gossip, and eat Indian food on 6th St. One night, after some dark beers and somozas, I said with great conviction, "I want to meet the Dalai Lama." Gary immediately responded, "Let's do it. Let's go to India next year." The three of us hugged and laughed at our boldness and then began to plan a trip to Dharamsala, India, the Dalai Lama's summer residence. The planning took months of Gary's time. We would travel by train, stay with Indian families, and eat at ashrams. It sounded exciting and daring.

When the time came to buy an airline ticket, however, I said I couldn't go. I didn't even know why. I used the excuse of work and money, knowing it wasn't true. I was relieved to be staying home while Gary and Robert rode on crowded trains and brushed their teeth with bottled water. My two friends toured India and had a private audience with the Dalai Lama while I remained in New York and taught computer minutiae to employees who hated their jobs.

The next trip I managed to avoid was a year later. Gary decided to return to India with a group. About 15 people signed up, myself included. Two months prior to leaving, we all gathered for introductions and it was clear the group had problems. There were heated debates about accommodations, transportation, and what to wear. After one person said he could only tolerate American food, people started dropping out, myself included. Gary ended up going by himself.

The third and fourth trips I passed on were with Robert. I was too busy working or moving or beginning a relationship or ending one. I was never short of excuses, though somewhere in my heart I did want to take the trip. Just not yet.

Last year, Robert and I once again started talking about going to India. We would stay in Benares for two weeks, then travel to Rishakesh. I definitely wanted to go, I told Robert, trying to convince myself.

As we started to make plans, my fears increased daily. I worried about getting along with Robert. He would probably wander off and leave me alone—something Gary said happened on their trip. And Robert wanted to stay longer than I did. How would I get to the airport without him? What if my 95-year-old mother got sick and needed to contact me? What if I got sick? A lot of people get sick in India. I'd read once in a guide book that a few tourists are killed each year by Indians who pretend to be cab drivers and then take the unsuspecting tourists to remote areas to rob, rape, and torture them.

Finally I faced the truth. This was going to end up like the other four trips. I was not going to go. I told Robert and cried with frustration.

The next day I felt the calm one feels after almost drowning, and realized that I did indeed want to go to India but could not handle the fears I associated with the trip. I am an avid reader of New Age literature and decided to ask the Universe (what and whoever that might be) to help me get to India. I said, "I am tired of trying to get to India. I am leaving it up to you. Just get me there. Spare me the details."

Soon after my pleas to the unknown, my friend Dick called. His partner Ellen was leading a group of women to India and two people had dropped out. Would I like to go? I had the weekend to decide. I called my friend Lynn to see if she wanted to join me. She said, "Life is short. I'll do it." Within a week, I had an airline ticket, an appointment for immunization shots, and an official Indian Visa.

It was a wonderful trip filled with learning, spirituality, and a reawakening of my own aliveness and humor. Hands down, I was the funniest and most irreverent person on the trip—the part of me I often buried inside a thousand fears.

When I returned, I realized that my trip to India was not about India at all. It was about admitting fear and taking the next step anyway. What I needed to learn in India I'd learned way before landing in New Delhi.

FAVORITE NATURAL ENVIRONMENTS

In the fall of 1993, I rode Amtrak's Empire Builder from Chicago to Portland, Oregon and back again. On the return trip, right after leaving Glacier National Park, we passed through Flathead National Forest in Montana. I was sitting with my fellow passengers in the Superliner car, all of us quietly gazing out the floor-to-ceiling windows. Suddenly, a rush of enormous pines, glistening creeks, and slanting sunlight came into view. In that instant, my eyes filled with tears. No words, no thoughts, just tears.

Truth is, I've felt drawn to many natural landscapes over the years: the Midwest prairie at dusk in full bloom; the frozen beauty of the northern forests; the coast of Maine; and the mesas of New Mexico.

But that crying thing, while riding the train through that dense wall of green, the light playing on the water—now that had never happened before. Or since.

Following are 4 writing prompts to help you revisit your favorite natural places

For the ***first,*** make a list of all those faraway natural places and landscapes that move and inspire you, maybe even make you cry. Choose just one and describe it in detail, using the sentence prompts I see, I hear, I smell, I touch, I taste. Write randomly and in no particular order. Just bring back as many scenes and images of yourself in this place as you can *through your senses*. See what stories from your time in this place emerge and tell one of them.

And then some: Do the above exercise with one of your favorite local landscapes: an urban garden; mountain switchback or prairie path; nature preserve; river, lake or ocean shore.

And then some more: Write about your childhood experiences in natural landscapes. Use the focused freewrite and sentence prompt "I remember" to recall as many of those places and stories as you can.

And then just one more: Spend time in a local natural environment that you've never been to. This can be a preserve, river path, botanical garden, bird sanctuary—any nearby natural place. Spend at least 30 minutes there, then sit some place comfortable and write about what you saw, heard, smelled and touched there. Don't worry about the order of this description; just get down as many details as you can. In the process, see what you discover about your preferences for specific natural settings. Think about what experiences might explain those preferences. Describe one in more detail.

From the Trenches

Jean sees a favorite natural place in a new light

My brothers and I were on a pilgrimage to see our family's summer cabin in winter. But after climbing the island's snow-covered bank, our excitement gave way to sadness. At first glimpse, the familiar gathering spot looked a desolate, lonely place.

When we stomped inside my feelings of estrangement intensified. It was as if the cabin was holding its breath. Standing in the front room, snow melting off my boots, I felt like an intruder, an uninvited guest.

Yet aside from a few seat cushions stowed away to prevent mouse attacks, the room was as it had always been. My grandfather's fishing poles were still propped up by the front door, his ancient metal tackle box next to them. The fraying olive-green rug occupied the center of the main room. The antique wicker chairs still faced the center of the rug, as if waiting for the return of summer, the time when we'd be together again talking about blueberry picking or reading or listening to the loons' haunting laughs.

That's the difference, I thought. On this bitterly cold day I was missing the pleasing sounds of summer: the waves slapping my younger brother's rowboat; children laughing as they leapt off the dock; the low-pitched drone of a fishing boat trolling close to shore.

We left the cabin, trudged through the white woods to the island's little lake, and ventured to the middle of the frozen expanse. We were enveloped in total silence, a sensation I'd never experienced before. I love the city, but the frequent intrusions of sudden, loud noises are disturbing. As my awareness of the silence grew, my entire body relaxed.

When we returned to the cabin for one last look, my feelings had changed. Instead of forlorn, the cabin now seemed peaceful, as if asleep. It had about it a hushed stillness, a refreshing pause before summer's lively activity. As we began our descent down the bank to the lake, I realized how much I loved that cabin—and this place—more than I'd ever known.

Favorite Built Environments

In the mid-1980s, I found myself getting antsy and needing a change. So with little sense and even less planning, I left Chicago and moved across country to Santa Fe, New Mexico. I'd never been to Santa Fe, but I liked the way it looked on a map, nestled up there in the Sangre de Christo mountains. A lifelong flatlander, I especially like saying, "Sangre de Christo mountains."

Soon after I arrived and hastily rented an apartment, I knew this particular plan wasn't going to work. As beautiful and exotic a place as Sante Fe is, I found myself dreaming nightly about the Newberry Library, a research library back in Chicago, missing it terribly, though I'd barely spent time there. It's a handsome building, dark brick and glass, and sits on a tree-lined street across from a small leafy park on the city's exclusive Gold Coast.

But more than the architecture and location, it was the interior mix of light, wood, and marble that symbolized what the library meant for me, stranded as I was out there in the arid southwest: urbanity; humane letters and learning; the life of the mind—all the things I valued represented in one solid but unimposing structure.

I left Santa Fe not long thereafter and returned to Chicago, where over the years I've became a frequent habitué of the Newberry Library, one of my favorite built places.

Following are 4 writing prompts to help you write about your favorite built environments

For the ***first***, make a list of those favorite built places near where you live—public places you enjoy being in, feel good in, even if you're not sure why. These can include restaurants, cultural centers, sports arenas, bookstores, coffeehouses, churches, libraries, taverns—any public built space you look forward to spending time in.

Then select one place, and begin to describe its features.

What do you see, hear, smell, touch, even taste while there? In the process, see if you discover any memorable experiences that occurred in this place. Record one.

And then some: Turn this exercise on its head and make a list of your least favorite places. Select one, and in no particular order, write down all the images and scenes from this place, particularly those that might explain why this is one of your least favorite places.

And then some more: Describe a favorite built place that you've visited on your travels. In the process, see what memories emerge, then write down one of the more interesting ones.

And then just one more: Think about those mundane places that are part of your everyday life: airports and train stations; grocery, hardware, and convenience stores; auto repair shops and laundromats. Are there any good stories lurking there?

Other Peoples' Homes

In 2002, three of my favorite places were lost to me: a quaint little inn I frequented in southern Wisconsin; my friends' home in New York City; and my niece's lovely starter house in suburban Chicago.

The inn was bought by a developer, torn down, and replaced with a row of prison-like apartment buildings. The homes were sold as part of the inevitable moving on so many of us do these days.

I'd begun visiting my friends' Manhattan apartment in 1994. Rose and Jake had moved there from Georgia in the fall of that year, the result of a job transfer. It was the second floor of a lovely old brownstone on the city's Upper West Side. I went there two or three times a year, for the better part of the eight years they owned it. In early 2002, my friends sold it and moved to a smaller place across town.

I have many wonderful memories of the three of us in that brownstone, including leisurely Sunday breakfasts out on their terrace and long conversations in front of the fireplace. One of those conversations is forever etched in my memory, a particularly poignant one that occurred weeks after 9/11. Rose worked just blocks from the World Trade Center and had witnessed much of the devastation following the terrorist attacks.

Following are 2 writing prompts to help you write about other peoples' homes

For the ***first***, begin with a list of those homes of friends and family members that you have spent some considerable time in as an adult. As you make this list, be aware of the pleasant images that come to mind of your experiences there. When you are finished with your list, begin to describe one of those experiences in more detail. See where the writing leads you.

And then some: Now start writing down images of unpleasant experiences associated with someone else's home. See what particular stories emerge from those, and record one of them in more detail.

From the Trenches

Marilyn writes about a wonderful room in her friend Kirk's house

I've been covetous of Kirk's bedroom since the first grand tour of his Chicago single-family. This room floats in a second floor dormer with mountain retreat pine flooring and white wainscoting. The bed is huge, a king, draped with a handmade spread he lugged back from Sardegna, bought from a street vendor and weighing about 30 pounds. A dust-free stillness showcases nicely-placed antiques; a window/door with the promise of a balcony flashes tree tops and sky with a disorienting, imaginative sense of place.

So tonight I find myself in his bed surprised that I got here after years of longing for the deep rest of his room, not knowing how that would ever happen. It's pitch black, and the glow-in-the-dark nail polish makes me gasp before I realize they are my own fingers dancing in the air before me. Maria laid a thick coat of polish on them—slumber party antics on this Halloween night.

It was the "girls" and Kirk. He fully takes care of us—food, drinks, poker, and pay per view. He's giddy and giggly and happy for the company because he's just left his found-out-cheating boyfriend. I initially resisted because I was wrestling nagging agoraphobia at the thought of a fitful night of tumbled blankets and the probability of the couch. Crabby Appleton.

But here I am in the place I never thought attainable, lying in the farthest corner of Kirk's bed, smiling and closing my eyes. I sink more comfortably than I ever thought possible. And what follows is a sleep so refreshing that I will be in the same exact pose come morning. No thrashing, no problems with the temperature, no noise, no bathroom breaks, no battle for covers from another bed partner, just pure slumber in the arms of alien comfort that may just rival any future experience.

The high thread-count sheets, the pillow top and fluffy down under my head and all because I spoke up for the bedroom upstairs. How did I manage that? So unlike the recent girlfriends' weekend getaway to a five-bedroom in South Haven. Pregnant Lou got the first floor queen. Judy and interloper Sheryl nabbed the first floor twins. Tina claimed the second floor double with a thump of her suitcase on the bed, and I was left to wander the house, avoiding the last two available beds—the first in a room with snoring Martha and the second in a bedroom with flatulent Janet, who managed to stink it up real good while the rest of us stayed up late watching "Susperia." By 4 a.m. I settled for the living room couch and was awoken at 6 a.m. by the first early bird riser.

But tonight is new. A deep healing. Enchanting. Because I used my voice. "Who wants the upstairs bedroom?" I do!

Nasty Places

In 1985, after getting accepted into graduate school, I signed up for some refresher writing courses the summer before my official academic life was to begin. In one of them, our first assignment was to go someplace we'd normally avoid and write a short journalistic piece about it.

With a slight sense of foreboding, I set out on a steamy Sunday morning in July for a gathering of New Age enthusiasts. I'd seen ads for the event in a local paper, and, were it not for the pressure of the writing deadline, would have certainly steered clear of it. But when I arrived at the hotel where the meeting was scheduled, I learned that it had been cancelled.

Now what? I wondered, standing on the south end of Chicago's Michigan Avenue, the sun beating down in earnest. I was starting to feel a little cranky: summer is not my favorite season; I had a writing assignment due in 24 hours; and I'd no idea what to write about.

Suddenly, off in the distance came the faint pulsing sound of rock music. It was just 9 am, for gawd's sake, where could it be coming from? Then I realized I was just blocks away from the Taste of Chicago, an annual outdoor food orgy that draws millions of people downtown each summer. For a sun-averse, claustrophobic introvert who loathes huge sweaty crowds, it was the worst possible place to be that morning. Perfect.

Off I marched, pen and paper in hand, eager to record every miserable moment.

Following are 3 writing prompts to help you tell some nasty place stories

For the ***first,*** make a list of places you normally try to avoid. As you're doing so, think about what makes you uncomfortable and cranky about these places. These should not be dangerous or scary places, but the kind you'd prefer not to hang out in—for whatever reason. Try to be as specific possible when making your list—not "big summer festivals with crushing numbers of people inhaling huge amounts of food," but "The Taste of Chicago."

Now pick one of these places, go there, and take lots of notes, jotting down what you see, hear, smell, and so on. Immediately afterwards, go sit in a more pleasant environment, then record your nasty place experience.

And then some: Write about an experience you had while in a dangerous or scary place. Include how you wound up there—and how you got out.

And then some more: Now go to one of the nasty places from your past, but this time in your memory. Put the phrase "Nasty Places from Childhood" at the top of the page and use the focused freewrite and sentence prompt "I remember." Describe the images and scenes from these places. See if they lead you to a particular story you'd like to tell.

From the Trenches

Loretta writes about a nasty place made less nasty by the person who led her there

The Sisters of Mercy, an order of nuns who help the poor, were delivering Thanksgiving dinners to families in some of Chicago's worst housing projects. This particular year, they needed volunteers to join them. I'd been warned about these places, but I took it all in with the naivety of a middle-class kid from a predominately white neighborhood, and signed up.

Thanksgiving morning arrived in its cold gray overcoat. I drove out of my neighborhood of well-tended lawns and swept alleys and joined a small group of girls in front of the Sisters' modest brick convent not far from the projects. Everyone was dressed in grubby clothes. A few wore their high school sweatshirts.

Our little band—teeny, tiny Sr. Agnes Marie and six high school girls in a blue beat-up van—made our way to the corner of Division and Halsted, an area known at the time for violence. But no alarms went off, no concerns about our safety.

We approached the first of ten places we would visit that day. The streets were vacant. Not a single person was walking or driving by. There was nothing but remains all around us: the remains of a swing set, of an old car, of a front lawn. Not one tree stood in that barren landscape.

Sr. Agnes instructed each of us to grab groceries and a bag containing a silver carton from the van. I could smell the aroma of turkey and gravy escaping from the carton's seams. Sister

Agnes carried nothing but the list of families and her keys.

"We won't be using the elevator," she said casually, as we started our climb up the first six flights. The stairwell was filled with rancid air: the smell of urine and stale food. This gray day now seemed brilliant compared to the shadowy darkness. The stairs were decaying; there was graffiti everywhere. It was impossible to read what any of it said, but the message was clear: stay away. With only a single uncovered light bulb on three of the floors to guide us, our progress was slow. But Sister Agnes moved up the stairs with an air of expectancy, as if we were visiting her very best friend.

Chapter 5

More Life Experiences

In addition to people and places, our stories are always about certain subjects—those "categories of experience" that are the focus of much of our day-to-day life. These include the universal themes of love, loss, and survival—and those more prosaic events having to do with work, money, and the weather. These subjects are one more source of our important stories.

The exercises and contributor submissions that follow will help you tell stories about particular subjects in your life.

Weather Stories

I remember teaching a workshop in Chicago on one of the coldest nights in the city's recorded history. It was scheduled on a Monday in January at a bookstore up the street from where I lived. The bookstore owner, a worried sound in her voice, called earlier in the day, asking if I was sure I wanted to hold the workshop; she too was listening to the hourly weather reports that predicted an evening low of *minus* 25 degrees. I told her I shared her concern, but that people were still calling throughout the day to register.

By the time we gathered at 7 pm, the store's large plate-glass windows had frosted over, and the bathrooms were unusable—the water pipes had frozen. But 10 of us intrepid writers sat huddled on folding chairs in a warm circle, most with our coats on, and for two hours wrote and talked about writing. I can see us there still, our soft laughter punctuated by short bursts of frosted breath.

This is one of my favorite cold weather stories. I have hot weather ones as well. And also stories about Chicago winds so fierce that migrating birds took refuge on high-rise ledges. And of blizzards that raged sideways down the Magnificent Mile. And of ghostly fogs off Lake Michigan. And so on.

Following are 3 writing prompts to help you tell your weather stories

For the ***first***, use the freewrite technique, the focus "Weather Stories," and sentence prompt "I remember" to recall your lifelong weather stories. Keep writing until a particularly interesting one emerges, then write about it in more detail.

And then some: Tell a really dramatic weather story. One of mine would be the night my family and I were driving through a major blizzard in northern Indiana, on our way east for the Christmas holidays. Visibility was in inches; there were trucks with major tonnage lying moribund in the ditches on either side of us. I remember sitting in the back seat, eyes closed, barely breathing, willing my nephew to keep us on the road. (He did.)

And then some more: Now take each of the four seasons—summer, fall, winter, and spring—and do a focused freewrite for each, using the sentence prompt "I remember." Go as far back in time as you can remember. Stay with specific images in the writing until one leads to a particular story.

From the Trenches

Joan finds inspiration in a sudden ice storm

It began quietly on Monday and continued through the next two days. With the temperature holding near the freezing mark, the rain quickly froze on the trees and bushes. The snow in the backyard was crusted with ice.

My husband and I, along with our two teenage daughters, had just moved into our new house a few days earlier. It was on a quiet street, surrounded by large oak trees. The conservancy park behind us seemed like a continuation of our yard.

Then, on Thursday, March 4, when the full force of the storm swept across southern Wisconsin, the power went out. Far from settled, we searched through boxes and unfamiliar closets until we found flashlights, candles, and extra blankets.

The trees cut down to make room for the house were now stacks of logs ready to provide warmth. The two fireplaces in the house that had seemed such a luxury were immediately put to use. We kept the fires burning, and with extra layers of clothing were almost warm.

Darkness came early. We gathered around the fireplace to talk and read by candlelight. The branches of the huge oak tree at the back of the house were heavy with ice. The increasing wind caused the branches to scrape back and forth across the roof, and we worried that one might break off and come crashing through.

After four days the power came back on. We had survived with no major damage, only minor inconveniences. I wrote the following poem to capture my experience of this magnificent storm:

The Ice Storm - 1976

In the night
rain freezes.
The wind rises.
Oak branches
heavy with ice
scrape across the roof.
Inside, warmed by the fire
we read by candlelight.

Holiday Stories

Whether you embrace them, ignore them, or run as fast as you can in the other direction, the holidays make for great stories. These are the annual occasions—Thanksgiving, Christmas, Hanukah, New Year's—when whether you like it or not, the family is gathering and you're expected to show up. Thus is the stage set for good times, much laughter, high drama, hot, angry tears—in other words, the full catastrophe.

Some of my more memorable holiday stories include a niece stomping off in the middle of Thanksgiving dinner; a former boyfriend showing up unannounced at Christmas; and celebrating New Year's Eve at a tiny Brazilian restaurant in New York. There was one Christmas I traveled to North Carolina to escape family, and another when I flew to California to be with them.

Some holidays I boycotted altogether, binging instead on movies, while on others I rushed to sit among the patchwork quilt of my family. But however I spend my holidays, I usually end up with a fistful of good stories.

Following are 3 writing prompts to help you tell your holiday stories

For the ***first,*** make a list headed "Holidays" and fill it in with all the holidays you typically celebrate throughout the year. Include not only the usual suspects—Thanksgiving, Christmas, Hanukkah, New Years—but also those appropriate to your own family traditions and culture. Then pick one holiday and use the focused freewriting technique and the sentence prompt "I remember" to recall all the images and scenes associated with this holiday. In the process, see if there's a particular story you'd like to record in more detail. And as with all the exercises in this book, try not to avoid any unpleasant or painful holiday stories.

And then some: Birthdays are particular kinds of special holidays and deserve writing exercises of their own. For this one, use the same focused freewrite and sentence prompt to recall the details from one of your many birthday celebrations. See where the writing takes you.

And then some more: The giving and receiving of gifts is part of many of our holidays and birthdays. For this exercise, make a list of all the gifts you remember both giving and receiving over the years, including whom they were from or to. Then pick one that you think might lead to a really good story, and write about it.

Work Stories

I was raised by a man who graduated from high school in 1929, the year of the infamous and devastating Crash. When I learned this about my father, suddenly everything fell into place, explaining his near hysteria every time I casually quit one job and sailed easily into another. He'd taken a job right out of high school with a company he stayed with for 40 years. I, on the other hand, raced like some prairie wildfire through an endless succession of jobs and careers: mailroom clerk, secretary, waitress, social worker, college instructor, and office temp.

I worked for a shower curtain company, three universities, a political campaign, a beauty supply company, two hospitals, a half-way house for the mentally ill, a camera store, and an upscale restaurant before finally settling down as a writer and a teacher.

Not surprisingly I've acquired some pretty good work stories along the way, not only about the getting and quitting of jobs, but also of bully bosses, psychotic colleagues, and office romances gone (real) bad.

Following are 3 exercises to help you tell some of your work stories

For the ***first***, make a list of specific jobs you've held since becoming an adult, no matter how long they lasted, or how insignificant they were. Pick any one on your list and describe where and when you performed this job, and who your colleagues and bosses were. Then describe yourself doing the job, as if someone had a camera trained on you while you were working. See what stories that leads you to.

And then some: Make a list of all the bosses you've had in your jobs. Then pick one and use the character sketch to bring this person to life on the page. What does s/he look like? What are his or her major traits and quirks? What are some of the more interesting interactions you had with this person? Write about one of those.

And then some more: Write about a particularly awful job—or about losing a job, quitting, getting fired, or being unemployed. Do more describing than reflecting, at least at first. You want to tell a good story about a negative experience vs. merely writing down your feelings about it. Let the details in the story do the main work of conveying those.

From the Trenches

Vashti describes the emotional experience of being fired

I found out I was going to be fired when reading an e-mail while half a world away. I felt sick and out of control.

When I got home from vacation, she called to ask me to meet with them. I refused.

"You're going to fire me, aren't you?" I asked over the phone.

"Yes," she answered.

"Just tell me now. I'm not coming in for this," I replied.

I cried. She cried. I hung up and threw the phone across the room. No real explanation, but I knew. It's a familiar story: people with power gave me up to save their own skin.

These were not just my supervisors; they were my colleagues and my friends. We'd all built this organization together, spending long hours fighting the "bad guys." We were with each other more than with our families. I saw their children as newborns in the hospital and they were my heart.

Now I had 24 hours to comply with the separation agreement they'd worked on with their lawyer: What they would say to the press. What I could say to the press. All face-saving manipulation of the truth, either way.

The computer I used for six years had to be returned. But so much of the contents were mine. I had to remove the personal data and transfer it to a new computer. It took many hours and I was under tremendous pressure. They accused me of stealing their information.

I felt alone and sad. My job was who I was in the world: a passionate advocate for the voiceless. My reputation. I worked so hard. My livelihood. My career. My life. And they took it away. My friends did.

I got an attorney. It was nearly impossible to think clearly through the emotional smog surrounding me. Do I let them control me for one month's severance pay? They changed the locks on the office door. I found that out on a Sunday when I went with family and a van to pack up my things. Soon I'll forget the anger and humiliation I felt when I put my key in the door and it wouldn't turn.

I went through all but one of the stages of grief: denial, anger, bargaining, and depression. The acceptance took months. But I was job-hunting the very next day. I am resilient—all survivors are. I've been fired before. It usually resulted from my speaking out. Often it's a principled stand. Sometimes it's not knowing when to stop speaking. I'm learning. I'm growing. I'm forgiving.

Stories About Games & Sports

This morning at my local coffeehouse, I got to talking with a fellow habitué about pinochle, a card game we both remembered from childhood. That got me thinking about other games I played while growing up: canasta, hearts, Monopoly, Pick-up Sticks, and the ever-popular Cootie. Then there was bid whist, a card game I learned to play during my freshman year at college—a state university out on the Illinois prairie.

I am sitting down in the basement smoker of our freshman dorm, the only white girl at a table of four African-Americans. It's midnight, maybe 2 a.m., probably a week night, a night I should be upstairs studying along with my more serious roommates. But I love playing cards, and this game looks pretty interesting. More important, I never knew any black people while growing up in my all-white suburb and I'm curious. These girls seem friendly and welcoming as I approach their table, and so when they invite me to join them, I sit right down.

Over the next several weeks of these late-night diversions, I will become a passable bid whist player, a feat my parents will celebrate with less enthusiasm than I. And though my knowledge of history and mathematics doesn't advance appreciably during this time, I have learned a fun card game, made some new friends, and expanded my worldview just a bit.

Following are 3 writing prompts to help you tell your sports and games stories

For the ***first,*** make a list of the board and card games you've played throughout your life. Stop when an interesting scene or image comes to mind. Then describe that scene and its circumstances, and, as always, see where the writing takes you.

And then some: Do this same exercise about the sports you've participated in over the years. Begin with a list of the kinds of sports—baseball, golf, tennis—then take one and name the people you played with. Let that exercise lead you to a particular sports story.

And then some more: Tell a story about those games or sports you've played with children—or watched them play with each other. Begin by making a list that links the child with his or her game or sport, i.e., William and soccer, Megan and Scrabble, and so on.

From the Trenches

June, a long-time Chicago Cubs fan, describes her experience at a Japanese baseball game

The deal was made with a shady-looking guy who correctly guessed our desperate situation. We conducted our transaction just outside the gate, crouching down and whispering, quickly handing over the cash. A drug deal? No! We had just paid a scalper 20,000 yen, or roughly $200, and now our family of four could experience the Japanese love for America's favorite pastime: baseball.

In 2005, my husband Steven and I traveled to Japan with our two young daughters and were lucky enough to visit the city of Kobe when the Hanshin Tigers were in town. They were hosting the Tokyo Giants at Koshien Stadium that warm summer night, and the crowd of 50,000 diehard fans was humming with excitement over the sold-out game. More than humming, actually. The noise level at a Japanese ballgame is absolutely deafening. The home team and visiting team each have their own cheering sections. There are cheers for every player that comes up to bat, and the fans chant them in unison, while smacking miniature plastic bats in rhythm. These bats are used for other purposes as well. When the Tigers' big slugger was intentionally walked, the lady next to me, obviously a Tigers fan, expressed her outrage by shouting and whacking her bats mercilessly on the fence.

Somewhere behind me a drum beat out a

loud and rhythmic boom-boom-boom. Two men in the stands, dressed in brightly colored Happi coats and wearing white gloves, were coordinating the cheers for the Giants. One of them jumped up and down frantically, like he was attached to a spring, and blew non-stop on an ear-piercing whistle, pi-pi-pi. Then, suddenly, when the half-inning was over and the Tigers came up to bat, the cheering and noise around us stopped. This was Japan, after all, and it is rude to cheer or boo when the opposition is up. Or maybe they were just exhausted from all that shouting and jumping and needed to catch their breath?

Now, from the opposite side of the stadium, it was the Tigers fans' turn to make some noise, and wave a huge flag from the stands. Even though we weren't in the "official" Tigers cheering section, there were plenty of Tigers fans where we sat, like the lady next to me who screamed and clapped her bats incessantly.

No hot dogs or Cracker Jack at a Japanese ballpark. Instead, I got a bento, a box lunch, with rice and fried pork cutlet. I was disappointed though. Like most baseball park food back home in Chicago, it was overpriced and mediocre. Maybe I should've gotten the curry rice instead. Or better to do what some other fans do—bring their own bento, no doubt purchased at a convenience store on the way to the park.

During the seventh-inning stretch, everyone in the stands released long, skinny balloons, punctuating the night sky with bright flecks of green, orange, and blue. Like fireworks, without the big bang.

The Tigers went on to win over the Giants,

and the player who made the winning run was honored afterwards. The two Tigers mascots, To-Lucky and Lucky, ran out and cavorted around the field. They were, of course, two people wearing tiger costumes: To-lucky, the boy tiger, and Lucky, in her Tigers skirt, the girl. Everyone sang the official Tigers song (which we didn't know) to celebrate the victory, and then it was time to go.

We all spilled out into the night. Everyone was happy and excited, except, understandably, the Giants fans. Their cheering section made a quick and quiet exit. The souvenir stalls were packed. Just like back home, the fans sported pin-striped jerseys, only with names like Kanemoto, Imaoka, Yano. And Tigers headbands with little striped furry ears were very popular with female fans. At one of the stands, I stopped to buy a towel, the long thin ones that the fans proudly drape around their necks, with the logo of the Hanshin Tigers. As a Cubs fan, it's easy to feel an affinity with a team that has won the Japan Series only once.

What If? Stories I Wish I Could Tell

You can't reach a ripe middle age without some regrets for roads not taken or dreams unfulfilled: the career you didn't pursue: the romance you let go; the risks you considered but avoided. These all constitute the stories we'll never tell—except, of course, in our imaginations.

For me, some of these "what if" stories include joining the Peace Corps; marrying that nice stable guy from Chicago; living in New York City; being a literature professor at Oxford; having children. Who would I now be, I wonder, had I lived even one of those lives? Would I be recognizable as myself? Or would these different experiences have made me a wholly different person?

What about you? Any "what if" stories lurking in your imagination?

Following are 3 writing prompts to help you tell your "What if?" stories

For the ***first***, start with a list of your unlived stories—those people, places, and events that might have become part of your life story but didn't. Select just one and create an imagined story, one that could have happened had you followed a particular path, made one choice instead of another.

In the writing, try not to get bogged down with all the reasons why you chose or lived otherwise, or with regret that you didn't. Simply turn the clock back, set the stage, and walk onto it. Where and when is it? Who's there with you? What's happening? "I get accepted into the Peace Corps and……" "I accept Bob's marriage proposal and…." Stay in the present tense in this exercise, open up your imagination, and create this parallel life in writing. See what you discover in the process.

And then some: Now try this exercise with options over which you had no control. For instance, what stories might you tell if you'd been born in a different decade or century? Of a different race or in a different culture? Who would you be if you had different parents? Or were a child prodigy in music? As with the previous exercise, let your imagination loose and write about the life you might have lived in these invented circumstances.

And then some more: Often our early life takes a dramatic turn through the loss of a loved one—a parent, sibling, or friend—whether through divorce, abandonment, or death. We might wonder what our life would've been like had that person remained a part of it. Do a writing exercise in which you bring your own lost friend or family member back in your life and imagine how it would be altered as a result.

From the Trenches

Parul writes a very sad "what if" story

It is the summer of 2000. I am sitting on a bed in my parent's home, reading a novel when I hear the front door bell ringing.

My mom opens the door, "It's your friend, Shaina."

I hear the murmur of banal greetings, and get up with a sigh. Shaina enters my room. I've not seen her in two months; she looks thinner, darker and listless. I blurt out, "Are you sick?"

Her eyes, poignant and solemn, dart around the room, fixing on mine for a fraction of a second. She sways her head sideways.

"Please sit." She slowly sits down on the bed and stares at the floor. I hear her whisper, "I wanted to talk to you."

"Right, go ahead."

"There is this boy, my school friend, he...I thought..., I mean he said things and then...he said he is getting married to someone...he said, there is nothing between us and...."

I felt a gulp in my throat. We were in college for three years and I never knew there was a guy in her life. I get up, walk towards her and put my hand on her hand. "It is okay."

She bit her lips. I think she was holding back her tears.

"Do you want to talk more? I am here." I gently pat her hand.

She looks up with vacant eyes, "I think this is the end of the road for me. I want to die."

My heart beats faster. I squeeze my fists and cautiously ask her, "Do you have a plan?"

She nods without looking at me, "I will inject

a potent muscle relaxant in my veins. There is nothing for me on this earth now."

I promptly say, "Just wait here. I will be back."

I dash to talk to my mother who is in the kitchen and hastily explain everything to her, "Call a psychiatrist. It is urgent."

After a few minutes, Shaina, my mom, and I head to a nearby hospital. Shaina is very reluctant. She tries convincing me that she is fine and just needs to go home to rest. But I tell her to trust me. We reach the hospital. A psychiatrist thoughtfully listens to my story, and then takes Shaina into the exam room.

He comes out after some time and looks gravely at us, "We will admit her. She has a case of serious depression with suicidal tendencies. She has even arranged for a syringe and a bottle of succinylcholine chloride, a muscle relaxant."

My mom and I swiftly exchange glances, "Will she be ok?"

The doctor nods, "I am positive, she should come out of this. She has strong social support and has very positive signs of good prognosis." He pats my shoulder and smiles, "Don't worry. She is in good hands. Everything will be just fine."

Unfortunately, I didn't suspect the gravity of her condition when she came to my house that day, and so never made that call. Her depression went undiagnosed and she committed suicide on July 12, 2000.

Music/Film/Art-inspired Stories

A friend once suggested that a new relationship had promise if the couple shared musical tastes, whether country, classical, jazz, or rock. I don't know if I agree, but it's true that music touches us deeply—and might even rouse us to action. Such music—a romantic ballad, a haunting instrumental, or some raucous and raunchy rock—can also shake and rattle our memories.

The other day I was playing one of favorite CDs by the McGarrigle Sisters, the Canadian duo who sing their lovely harmonies in both English and French. Their rendition of Linda Ronstadt's "Heart Like a Wheel" suddenly transported me back 20 years, to the night I sat wrapped in the arms of a new paramour, that song playing quietly in the background. I not only saw this scene in all its intense detail, but recalled the thought I had in that moment: Ah, sweet paradise! My life is now complete.

Alas, both that night and the relationship came to a swift-enough end. But the sweet memory is still with me, brought back to life every time I hear "Heart Like a Wheel."

Following are 3 writing prompts to help you tell those stories inspired by music, art, or films

For the ***first,*** look through your catalog of CDs and tapes, then take out any favorite and play it. You want to be alone for this exercise—no distractions—and with at least 30 minutes to spare. Just sit and listen to the music and let all the scenes from those memories related to it play in your mind. When one of those music-inspired memories seems worth recording, take out your journal and begin writing.

And then some: Do this exercise after watching a movie that particularly moves or inspires you. Start by describing characters, actions, or scenes from the movie that were particularly compelling or provocative. As you do this, see what people and events from your own life bubble up in your memory. Then start to describe those.

And then some more: Do this same exercise after viewing a painting or photo at a public exhibit. Again this should be some visual art that touches you in some deep way, causes an emotional response that triggers some interesting memories.

For both the film and art exercise, make some notes immediately after viewing if you cannot complete the exercise shortly thereafter. Then later, before doing the exercise, read over your notes. This will help lead you to the personal stories related to these public works of art.

Animal Stories: Wild & Domestic

The dogs and cats I grew up with and owned as an adult have always been a big part of my life. The stories I've told—and continue to tell—about them are equal parts joyous and funny, painful and sad.

My wild animal stories are of a different order, though still dramatic and full of feeling. They include tracking a wolf pack in Northern Minnesota, driving through a bison herd during mating season in Montana, and being surrounded by rumors of mountain lions in Glacier National Park.

But my favorite wild animal story involves a pasta-loving mouse who'd found its way into my 2nd floor city apartment several years ago. Once I figured out that this little intruder was making regular visits to my kitchen, especially on the nights I cooked pasta, I decided to relocate him to one of our neighborhood parks. I can still hear the humane trap snapping shut the night I finally nabbed him, the startled mouse inside, and the lure—a single piece of cooked rigatoni—uneaten.

Following are 2 writing prompts to help you tell your favorite animal stories

For the ***first***, make a list of your wild animal encounters, from as far back as you can remember. Think of those times when you purposefully went looking for these creatures, when you accidentally stumbled upon them, or when they accidentally stumbled upon you. List your encounters with animals great and small—from the grizzly to the ladybug, from the ubiquitous to the rare. Pick one from your list and tell that story. Keep working your way down this list and keep adding to it. As with the kids in our lives, we can never have too many animal stories to tell.

And then some: Now tell a domestic animal story—one about your own pet, or perhaps someone else's. For this exercise, make a list of the names of these various dogs, cats, birds, horses, turtles, guinea pigs—any pet that you shared some part of your life with. My list would include, in no particular order, Stranger, Merry Christmas, Ed the Cat, Rollie, Reuben, Jelly, Cappy, Roddy, Ayla, Ron, and Mooey—among many, many others.

These animal stories will locate you in a specific time and place, but the action may be secondary. The emphasis in the writing might be on the relationship you had/have with these creatures—and on how that special bond enriched your life.

From the Trenches

Mary Lynne writes about Buddy the dog:

"Buddy" was a dog I first encountered at the animal shelter where I regularly volunteer. He had only been there a couple of days and, before that, he'd been fending for himself on the streets. I can only imagine how terrifying it was to be brought there and kept in a cage for 23-1/2 hours a day. The first time I saw him I noticed a warning note on the cage, telling people how frightened he was, and so how it might be difficult to get in and out of the kennel. Far from being a deterrent, this made me want to work with him all the more.

I opened the cage and, without making any eye contact, waited for Buddy to come to me. Before long, he did, head lowered, and tail tucked. I reached underneath his chin to let him acquaint himself with my hand, then clipped the leash onto his collar.

Once we got outside, he tended to walk several steps ahead of me. He didn't pull on the lead, as so many troubled dogs do, but walked just out of reach. Each time he got out in front, I silently stopped and stood my ground, and he immediately returned to my side.

While the shelter was being renovated, foster "parents" were needed to house all the dogs, and, without hesitation, I requested Buddy. When he arrived at my house, I let him check the place out, and he promptly found my own dog's bed, and made himself at home. Although he got along fine with my Golden Retriever, Pandora, Buddy didn't want to play with her in the first days.

It quickly became apparent that Buddy had been abused in his former life; this explained why he wisely kept out of reach of human hands while on lead. There were times when he thought he was "in trouble" with me and would crouch, then roll on his side in submission, awaiting punishment. I cannot imagine what kind of person had abused such a wonderful, affectionate creature and then put him out on the street.

I kept a record of the progress Buddy made each day he spent in my home. When he first arrived, he wanted to follow me everywhere and became extremely distressed every time I left the house. But within a few weeks, he accepted my departures with only a few barks to let me know his displeasure. I can't take all the credit for Buddy's recovery. With her antics, Pandora was able to persuade Buddy to play with her in just four days' time. I had never been able to entice him to play at the shelter. After a few weeks in my home, he even began retrieving a ball for me, although I suspect he did it more to make me happy than out of any love for the game.

In the end, a lovely couple adopted Buddy. They prepared their home for his arrival and kept in touch with me about how to resolve behavior issues, and to let me know how he was progressing. They gave him a new name along with a fresh start, and brought him for occasional play dates with Pandora and me. When I see him now, I see not only a dog who is fit, healthy, and well-loved, but one who no longer fears human strangers or ducks at the sight of a raised hand. This is what this dog has deserved all along.

From the Trenches

Donna tells her wild animal story

One summer I attended a “Women of the Earth” poetry class at a university field station in northwest Wisconsin. There was talk among the staff of a legendary black bear, an unofficial mascot named Bruce, who’d prowl the campus, which was more like a summer camp. Students slept in small log cabins and used pit toilets located in separate buildings. Reportedly, Bruce came around often at night, evoking apprehension about bathroom visits after dark.

A photo gallery in the director’s office showcased Bruce snooping around dumpsters, scratching against trees, and generally exploring the area. Most students hoped to get a glimpse of him—sort of.

During our second to last night, my classmates and I had the usual bonfire blazing on the shore of the lake. We sat there roasting marshmallows, star-gazing, discussing the day’s events, and bonding the way people do when immersed in a serene natural setting.

Gradually—though at first I thought it was my imagination—I became aware of a distant snort. Other than our voices and the gentle waves lapping the sandy beach, it was the only sound around for miles. I glanced across the campfire and noticed the same quizzical look on my instructor’s face.

“Shhh,” she finally whispered. We all listened as the snorts became louder, now accompanied by the sound of rustling tree leaves and heavy footsteps. No one wanted to appear afraid; we were professed nature lovers, after all. But suddenly we were all up on our feet. Finally someone said, "It must be Bruce," in a high-pitched tone that betrayed everyone's secret emotions.

My own heart was pounding. I wanted to see him, but then again didn't, at least not up this close. "Whatever you do, don't run," our instructor commanded in a hoarse and urgent whisper. My imagination ran wild as the snorting and footsteps came so close we could feel the vibrations. Whatever was making those sounds was approaching rapidly, and any second would burst out of the woods and into our camp site.

We all started inching backwards, too afraid to turn our backs on the approaching beast, and forced ourselves to retreat slowly up the hill toward the latrine, our cabins being too far away. Then, as we heard the creature finally burst through the trees, we all ran for dear life, gasping for breath as we found haven in the latrine.

Finally, someone got the courage to peek out of the doorway. We peppered her with urgent questions, "Is it Bruce? Is he coming our way?" Her sudden laughter slowly coaxed us all out of the building. There, standing in the clearing and snorting so heavily we could see his breath, was a huge and striking buck. He stayed for a few moments then disappeared back into the woods.

Later the next day, I thought about how our desire to be in the presence of big wild animals doesn't always square with our actions—especially when their appearance seems imminent. In the end, perhaps our two worlds really aren't meant to collide.

Stories About Food

Our food stories are found in lots of different settings: at home and the homes of others; during birthday and holiday celebrations; at fancy restaurants and fast-food joints; during picnics and parties; and while traveling.

As I think about these settings, several food memories come to mind:

Eating warm chocolate chip cookies fresh out of the oven on those few occasions my mother took to baking;

The goofy notes my father would slip into my school lunch bag whenever he packed it for me, including those he put *inside* the sandwiches themselves ("Help! I am being kept prisoner in a meatloaf factory!!");

The first time I, as a still-practicing Catholic in the '60s, ate meat on a Friday, thereby putting my mortal soul at risk. It was at La Posada del Rey, a dimly lit Mexican restaurant on what seemed the edgier side of town, and I was on my first date with an ex-seminarian.

But many of my most interesting food stories come from the five months I spent as a waitress (pardon me, *server*) at a swanky restaurant on Chicago's north side. One night a well-to-do patron casually tipped me a $100 bill following a very romantic dinner for two. Did I deserve it? Likely not, even though I was wearing a tuxedo *and* had finally mastered the fancy wine opener. But this fellow was trying to impress his much younger girlfriend, flinging lots of money around, and a bit of it just happened my way.

Following are 4 writing prompts to help you recall your favorite food stories

For the ***first***, make a list of those places that were and still are the settings for your own food stories. Include both public and private places, the familiar and strange, the cheap eats and Michelin three-stars.

After you make this list, pick one and in random order

write down all the images you recall from this place. When a particular incident or story emerges, describe it in more detail.

And then some: Now tell a funny food story using the freewrite technique and focus "Funny Food Stories." These stories might have to do with the food itself, the making and serving of it, or the people involved.

And then some more: Now use the same technique, but change the focus to "Ghastly Food Stories." These should be experiences where any number of things went very wrong.

And then just one more: Many of our food stories center around healing and reconciliation, some based in religious traditions, others not. Start with a list of those, then pick one to record in more detail. Pay particular attention to the restorative nature of the experience.

From the Trenches

Steve writes about a memorable meal while traveling

We spill out of the stuffy tour bus and cluster like startled chicks to see who will go where. We are in Gubbio, a medieval city in Umbrian Italy with huge baskets of tomatoes, peppers, and bunches of green, soft lettuce lining narrow brick streets. Three of us want the quintessential Italian lunch and peek around a shop door to inquire. A stout woman points to a gently curving road up the hill.

The steep road looks daunting as the friendly sun turns hot. Sweat dampens my white cotton shirt. I press on with my Greek-American friend Jim and the only woman who speaks fluent Italian, Rosemary.

There is no mistaking the welcome shade of the white canvas umbrellas at a stone farmhouse. A balding, white-haired man emerges to greet us. "Sit, sit....our food is the best in Gubbio. You want wine?" He disappears and we sit in the mismatched chairs while four dusty goats strain against the fence, sniffing us. A sweating wine carafe and rustic loaf of bread with black olive tapenade appear. The wine slakes our thirst while we tear at the rough crusty bread.

Our host eagerly describes a four-course meal while Rosemary translates for Jim and me. First, three bowls of dark linguini arrive, minced mushrooms are mixed with a hint of garlic in béchamel sauce, then swirled around the pasta. Butter-soft green lettuce leaves are then tossed before our eyes with a steady stream of olive oil and balsamic vinegar.

Crispy brown skin peels easily from the moist roasted duck. Thyme and ground sea salt are the only dressings for this perfectly cooked meat. We lick legs, breasts, and thighs, kissing the marrow from bones. I sit back and sigh, sipping the tart wine, feeling it slide down my throat.

We are far from home and the wine has softened our reticence. Jim says his wife is at home caught in a reverie of confusion over their marriage. Rosemary says her husband has come to expect these frequent escapes to her beloved Italy, a hard-won independence from a wealthy, powerful man. I am stunned daily by the unaffected beauty of Italian men with their half-grown beards, black leather shoes, and tight jeans.

Our chef, a round-cheeked, rotund woman with a thin-lipped smile, appears with raspberries spilling over lemon gelato and shot glasses filled with limoncello. We clap and Rosemary erupts with a litany of exuberant Italian gratitude.

We weave and bob down the pavement back to our bus. All will be well with our American lives and loves. We've had our way at the table with the finest of country Italian chefs.

Stories About Loss/Good-bye Stories

Loss and good-bye stories come in all shapes and sizes, from the trivial to the life-altering. We lose wallets and gloves; friends and loved ones; jobs and homes; our innocence and idealism. We lose money; we lose weight. We lose hope; we lose our illusions.

We say good-bye to neighbors; graduate from high school; send children off to college. We see familiar landscapes transformed, a healthy body damaged, a damaged body restored.

Some of our losses release us; some hobble us. Some good-byes are good riddances, setting us down a better path, while others may haunt us through the years.

But as the Greek philosopher Heraclitus said, you cannot step twice into the same river. And so we learn to accommodate loss, resign ourselves to its inevitability, though we may never be on friendly terms with the more serious and lasting good-byes.

Following are 4 writing prompts to help you tell your loss and good-bye stories

For the ***first,*** make a list of all of your experiences of loss and good-bye, both small and large. Include those that were ultimately good for you, as well as ones lastingly difficult to bear. Name names on this list, events and locations.

After you've made your list, put it away for a week. When you go back to it, review it for accuracy and completeness, i.e., should you add or delete any entries?

Then for the second part of the exercise, use the sentence prompt "What I notice about this list is...." to write down whatever thoughts come to mind as you look over your list. Think about the length of your list and the kinds of losses on it. Do you see any patterns? Does one type of loss seem to dominate? Keep using this prompt to reflect on what these accumulated losses mean to you, and on how they've played themselves out in your life. When a particular experience of loss arises in the writing, go on to record it in more detail.

And then some: Select from your list a loss that has been very beneficial to you in the long run, even if at the time it was hard to accept. Now tell that story.

And then some more: Describe a loss that remains difficult for you to accept. See what details best illustrate why this loss affects you still. Use the third person when telling this story. ("Bill was 55 when he was fired from his job of 30 years....")

And then just one more: Ernest Hemingway wrote that "the world breaks everyone, and afterwards, many are strong at the broken places." Surely our broken places include many of the losses we've sustained in our lives, whether of health, family, friends, jobs, faith, and even hope.

Make a list of what you consider to be your own broken places; go back as far in time as you can remember. As you work your way down this list, tell the stories behind those particular "places" that have made you stronger.

From the Trenches

Louise writes about what at first seems like a minor loss

I still feel a twinge when I think of the loss of my avocado-green travel umbrella. That was more than 30 years ago, and though I've owned dozens of similar umbrellas since, that one was special. Besides, I wasn't the one who lost it.

My family saw it as just an ordinary umbrella and didn't understand why I was so steamed when it was lost. I hardly understood it myself at the time. It wasn't as if we couldn't buy another umbrella. But this one had a unique easy-to-use design, and, frankly, I've never seen another like it. It had a two-piece collapsible handle that shortened or lengthened with a single press-and-thrust movement, and short, straight spokes that folded down simply when the umbrella was closed. I didn't have to wrestle with it as I do with the travel umbrellas of today, with their "automatic" opening mechanisms and tangle of multi-hinged spokes. No, I could put it to use at a moment's notice or easily pack it away. The umbrella was uncomplicated and straightforward, and its most important feature was that it was mine.

We were living in Southern California at the time, and one morning, I lent the umbrella to my 7-year-old stepson, Jimmy, to take to school. At the end of the day, Jimmy came home without the umbrella. I blew up. At the edges of my anger, I knew that Jimmy's failure to bring the umbrella home wasn't premeditated misbehavior. But in the middle of my outburst, I fixated on his forgetfulness and irresponsibility. What possessed him to be so careless with my personal belongings? It likely had something to do with his being seven years old, but I wasn't able to think along those lines at that point.

Unlike the umbrella, my life then was anything but uncomplicated and straightforward. For several years before the umbrella was lost, I'd been used to living an independent life, and to thinking of my possessions as my own. With no experience of children whatsoever, I'd married a year earlier, instantly becoming a full-time stepmother. I had to give up quite a lot in exchange for what I hoped would be familial bliss: a job I loved, a city I loved, and all the friends I loved who lived there. I didn't expect that I'd have to sacrifice the few things I owned, too, however mundane and inconsequential they might be. Maybe that's why I got so angry. Or maybe it was because of a growing awareness that adapting to marriage and motherhood meant acquiring a new sense of self, one without me and my stuff at its center.

And so the loss of my umbrella felt like the last straw among all of my losses. It wasn't, of course. Three decades and two more kids later, I can say that that loss was only the beginning of a long string of losses and sacrifices that dismantled my old sense of self bit by bit, forcing me to construct a new identity for the sake of my family. Along the way, I learned that family life has its own rewards. I don't really regret the loss of my old self now, but once in a while, the loss of my avocado-green travel umbrella still gives me a twinge.

Illness & Accident Stories

An awful lot of my accident stories took place while I was in motion: riding a bike; sitting in a car; walking on slippery ice; and, of course, roller skating.

But as I make this short list, the accident story I'm most drawn to tell is when I fractured my left wrist after scaling a barrier fence on Chicago's Oak Street Beach. Yes, this was way back in my wayward youth. I was on a date with a handsome soldier fresh from basic training, it was very late at night, and we'd been enjoying some sweet banana wine. And I just *had* to get to that part of the beach that was cordoned off.

I can still feel that rickety old fence give way as I fell down hard on the other side; still see the look on my father's face when he learned the next morning of my misadventure; still feel the weight of the itchy cast I wore throughout the blazing summer of 1966.

Following are 4 writing prompts to help you tell your illness and accident stories

For the ***first,*** make a list of your accident stories—but only of those that did not involve serious or tragic consequences. While not fun or problem free, these should be accidents that you survived and recovered from, no worse for wear, accidents you can maybe even laugh or joke about now. Now pick one of those stories to tell.

And then some: Then there are the more serious accidents that you were involved in, some of which may seriously affect you still. When you tell one of these stories, emphasize the person who was most helpful to you during this time. Begin with a list of people who were the major players in this story and select the most supportive from among them. Then use the character sketch technique to describe this person in more detail. How did they show their support of you? What did they do—or refrain from doing—that was helpful?

And then some more: Tell someone else's accident story, either minor or serious, even if you weren't directly involved in it. I'm thinking of a supervisor from one of my first jobs who'd been in a terrible car accident when she was 23 years old. It had left her a quadriplegic, totally dependent for her most basic needs on those who lived and worked with her. I can tell lots of stories about Peggy, many of which include *my* struggles to deal with her handicap.

And then just one more: Now tell some of your illness stories, both minor and serious. Use the freewrite technique and the focus "Illness Stories" and write without stopping for 10 minutes. Then see which of your illness stories you want to write about in more detail.

From the Trenches

Lois, a nurse, misdiagnoses her own injury following a fall

I don't usually invite blue-uniformed men into my bedroom. But that changed early one morning several months ago.

The night before, I'd fallen on a city sidewalk and thought I'd strained some ligaments in my right thigh. So before my husband left for work the next day, he'd placed my rolling desk chair next to my bed in case I'd need it. When I woke up in our 17th floor condo, I had to go to the bathroom. Normal enough. I inched my legs over the side of the bed. Fire-hot pokers shot through my right groin. I edged myself onto the chair and pushed backwards the 10 feet to the bathroom.

When I woke up the second time, I was still in the chair, half-way back to the bed. Cold sweat pasted my lavender knit nightgown to my limp body. I must have passed out. I'm a nurse, I should know.

Maybe I also should've known not to diagnose myself. After my fall, a police officer, a homeless man, and the shook-up couple behind us had all implored me to wait for an ambulance. With my husband's help, I struggled to stand, then slowly moved my right leg around in a circle. "See," I responded, "I have full range of motion. I'll be fine, just hail a cab."

My husband shrugged, "She's a nurse. You can't tell her anything."

Now, rising from the chair, I gripped my right thigh to distract me from the groin pain and tiptoed the five steps back to bed. A second later, my 30ish daughter called. I cried, "I'm so sick. Call Dad and have him ask the doorman to bring me up some juice." Maybe I was simply lightheaded.

Minutes later, Louis arrived, then handed me a glass of tomato juice, saying, "You don't look so good, Ms. R______"

I took a sip and upchucked a gallon in the top sheet I'd quickly cupped to form a basin. The dresser in front of me danced on the wall.

Louis held out the phone. "You better call 9-1-1."

Before I could press the three numbers, I deposited another quart of tomatoey liquid onto my husband's side of the bed. I wanted to even out the decorating.

When I hung up, I immediately heard sirens. They were coming for me. I felt silly—I'd never been an ambulance patient.

Next thing I knew six uniformed men had surrounded my bed. One asked what happened, another started an IV, a third asked where I kept my garbage bags.

I continued to urp into a garbage bag. Nurses don't behave this way, I told myself. But an hour later, I no longer felt silly for calling 9-1-1. The ER doctor told me, "I've got bad news. Your hip is broken."

FAMILY PHOTOS

Four years ago, while helping my father and stepmother move into a retirement home, I found a stash of my father's personal papers; they included an old photo wallet of my mother's. It was like finding gold. She had died in 1964—at 50—but was suddenly very much alive in that room and in that moment. I quickly leafed through the wallet and saw that only a handful of the plastic sleeves were filled—all the more reason to treasure the find.

Later that night, I carefully opened the wallet and pored over each of the six photos: one of my maternal grandparents; of my grandfather alone; two of my own high school pictures; one of my mother dressed for Halloween in a chicken suit; and finally the photo I was most curious about. Gathered in it were the major players in my mother's small family: her parents, sister and brother-in-law, and her grown niece, Betty, whom I know mattered to her more than anyone else in that picture. They are sitting close together on the slanting front lawn of a white frame house in Philadelphia, where my mother grew up. They look relaxed and merry, all collapsing into each other, arms slung loosely around shoulders.

Why had this picture been taken, I wondered? And what did it mean to my mother? I wanted to know the *story* behind this photo. I felt it might help me better understand the mother who died much too young, leaving me with an incomplete picture of who she really was.

Following are 3 writing prompts to help you write about your family photos

For the ***first,*** find a family photo that similarly intrigues you, one where you know the people in the photo, but have room to speculate about why they are all gathered together in it. As you look over this photo, think about how this one scene might illuminate your larger family story.

Begin by describing the photo—who's in it and where it

was taken. Then see what memories of your family come to life as you write.

And then some: Now find and describe a photo of yourself—either with other people or alone. Write about what was going on in your life at the time—both as you remember and imagine it. In the process, see if there's a particular story that you uncover from this period in your life.

And then some more: Ask a friend for one of his or her family photos, making sure it's of people unfamiliar to you. In doing the exercise, describe what you see in the photo then invent the story behind it. Share that fanciful exercise with your friend and see if there's any correspondence between his or her memory and your invention.

From the Trenches

Lisa contemplates a photo of her father

For years I've not taken any photos of my father. I am uncomfortable looking at them. Our estrangement is so deep that the intimacy of a photo feels embarrassing. The truth is that I do not know who my father is. And so it was awkward when, on a recent visit, my sister Maggie had her boyfriend take photos of us with Dad at the nursing home he'd been living at the past four months.

In the photo, Dad and I are inside his room looking through the window, where Joe stands outside holding the camera. Maggie is also outside, but standing by the window. And so while the three of us are posed together, we are separated by barriers. Dad sits hunched in his wheelchair, beard scraggly, eyes clouded with confusion. I stand next to him, having just washed his face and brushed his hair to make him presentable. Joe and Maggie are outside because they've just assembled the bird feeder we brought to draw Dad's attention outside the confines of his dark room. He used to be a bird lover and watcher.

This photo inserts a marker in a six month journey, one in which my father's health has deteriorated so rapidly that he can no longer live on his own. He needs help dressing, bathing, using the bathroom, and preparing his food. He can barely walk and stays in his wheelchair or bed most of the time. He suffers from depression and disconnection, neither of which is new, only more pronounced.

My sister and I have wanted for so long to be

close to Dad, but he doesn't seem to want that. I've never understood why. Maybe we intimidate him with our assertiveness and self-sufficiency. Or perhaps he just can't get close to others. Whatever the reason, it has mystified us for years.

My father is a time traveler – living in his head in the past. Every time I go to see him I ask what he's been thinking about, hoping to open a conversational door he might want to step through. Inevitably he says he's been thinking about his childhood or his brother or his parents and how hard they worked. He never says the things I want to hear: that he thinks about us – his daughters – or what it was like when we were growing up. Or how much he appreciates us or wishes we could spend more time together.

When I look at this image of the three of us, I know I will never really know my father. But I hold onto it; it may be the last one I have of him.

From the Trenches

Karen recalls the story behind a photo of herself as a young girl

Sorting through my Mother's belongings after she died in 2000, I found several old black and white photos, including one of myself in the summer of 1948, when I was five. I am sitting on the cement stupe stoop of the house next door, wearing a short-sleeved t-shirt and shorts, staring at the camera without a trace of a smile. My head is propped up by tightly clenched fists, my elbows resting on my knees. Though my face is partially hidden by the shadow of someone next to me, I can see the furrows on my brow. My body is tightly strung, though my eyes, deep and dark, cry out.

Why did my mother keep this picture of me? Did she feel guilty about the look in my eyes? Did she regret taking me from my father? He was a short, stocky German immigrant with thinning sandy hair, wire-rimmed glasses, and a broad smile that hid his cruelty. When my father would walk into the kitchen of our home, my mother told me I would wave my arms, wildly impatient, smiling radiantly and waiting for him to pull me from the high chair.

Three years before the picture was taken, my mother walked out of our house with only me and the clothes on her back, to go home to the attic flat where she'd lived with her brothers and mother.

My world split in two that day. No longer the beloved daughter, I was now a little adult in a world of strangers. My mother was distant, wrapped in her own world of disappointment and despair. My grandmother was short-tempered. The "boys," as grandmother called my uncles, got the best chairs in the living room, first dibs on the bathroom. We women shared the large back bedroom. I remember that dark room with my small cot shoved against the wall next to the double bed where my mother and grandmother slept.

As a fingered the photo, I recalled a story my mother once told me. One morning I was awakened by the voices of my mother and grandmother talking in the next room.

"I don't vant to take care of another child."

"What was I supposed to do, Mother? I couldn't live with him anymore."

"I told you he vould be trouble. I varned you."

"Karen woke up crying again last night. She knows we're talking about sending her away to boarding school," my mother said.

"Vat am I supposed to do vit the rest of my life? I don't want to be trapped all day in this small space vit her. I vant to get out, visit my friends, and play cards. I can't have Karen vit me."

"I will not send her away. I can't!"

A long silence punctuated my quiet sobs.

"Helen, we don't have to send her away. Mrs. Miller tells me her granddaughter goes to day school. Ve can send Karen to day school. I just need my time."

Then I heard footsteps headed toward the bedroom. I pulled the covers over my head and pretended to sleep. My mother opened the door and headed for the dresser, fiddling first with lipstick then a perfume bottle. I smelled Chanel #5 before I felt her sit on the edge of my cot. Her hand brushed my forehead as she straightened the covers. I yawned and opened my eyes. My mother leaned down and kissed me. "My little bunny is awake," she whispered in my ear. "Uncle Herbie is done in the bathroom. Off you go now and wash up. Breakfast is on the table."

Later that day, sitting on the stoop next door, I decided I could take care of myself. I didn't need my father—I didn't need any of them. Then my mother appeared with her camera. "Smile!" she entreated me. "Say cheese." I stared at the camera, holding myself as tight as I could.

Big Risk Stories

The French writer Andre Gide said, "One doesn't discover new lands without consenting to lose sight of the shore for a very long time." This is an apt, even comforting, metaphor for how adrift we feel whenever we leave our comfort zone and head into the Great Unknown.

But why do that? Why not just stay put in our cozy little life, even if we're not all that happy or satisfied with it? Likely because we hope that something better, maybe even amazing, awaits us in *terra incognito.*

And so our big risk stories describe those times we've left the familiar and safe and entered strange, but hopefully friendly, territory: a new relationship; a change in career; a move across the country, or the globe.

My own big risk tales include falling in love (and, even riskier, doing so more than once); quitting a safe civil service job at 41 to go back to school; submitting my writing for publication; and traveling alone in the desert Southwest for weeks on end.

Following are 4 writing prompts to help you write about the big risks you've taken in your life

For the ***first,*** make a list of your big risk stories. Think of risks you took in work, love, moves, travel and beyond. These are stories involving choices you made to go out on a limb in search of a way to enhance your life. Choose one of those stories and tell it, emphasizing what you had to lose ("the sight of the shore") in the process.

And then some: Tell a story about a big risk you took that did not pay off as you'd imagined it would. In the process, see if you can discover what this story taught you about yourself and the risk-taking process.

And then some more: Two of my big risk stories involved decisions that felt more like imperatives than real choices: ending a marriage and electing to have surgery for an early cancer. Each was more like walking a plank—no real option but to jump—than sallying forth with joy and optimism. Think of a similar kind of risk in your own experience—one that felt more like an imperative than a choice—and tell that story.

And then just one more: What big risk stories await you still? In the areas of love, work, and pure adventure? Make a list of those future risks you hope to take. Now imagine your way into one of these stories, and describe what happens. When you're finished with this exercise, make the to-do list that will set this big risk story in motion.

From the Trenches

Matt describes a very special kind of risk

I was 34, my wife, Bridgett, 33, when we sat and talked one evening about starting a family. I reminded her that we weren't getting any younger, and she quickly agreed. We'd been married for eight years, and the longtime refrain that we'd have kids in a "couple more years" had long since strained credulity.

We got pregnant right away—with twins. I should note that this joyful fact didn't reveal itself to us until the ninth month, a subplot that is one heck of a story of its own. Now, five years later, it's hard to conceive of what we were doing before Zachary and Maggie Rose arrived.

Shortly after they were born, I confessed to Bridgett that I'd thought parents could lay their kids in a neat little box, call "timeout," go get a nice Italian dinner, and enjoy the new blockbuster movie before strolling back home and resuming life as a parent. No problem.

Instead, parenthood has been a physical, emotional, and spiritual sparring match. We arrive at every decision—mundane or life-altering—by considering its effects on each other, on the kids, on our marriage: Who should go to the bread shop? Should I wear sandals or shoes? Should we have more children?

It's one thing to hear that there's nothing so difficult and rewarding as raising kids. But it's quite another to live it. That tired cliché doesn't begin to tell the tale.

Now, in those moments when I'm alone with the kids, the primary caregiver for the moment or afternoon or day, I'm reluctant to let them out of my sight for more than 20 seconds, especially hyper-adventurous Zach. To do so would be, well, risky.

Stories About Religion

My stories about religion usually center on my being raised in a "mixed" marriage. This was a really big deal back in the 1930s, when my Catholic father and Lutheran mother wed. But they were young and in love and imagined it would not matter that they were of different faiths. They were wrong, alas, and so for the most part, these are not happy stories. They reveal the fault lines in my parents' relationship, their religious differences serving as a sinkhole for their other troubles.

But after years of religion being such a wedge issue between them, something quite miraculous happened some 30 years down the line: my mother converted to my father's faith as she neared her death from breast cancer. In truth, I don't think it much mattered to her which institutional religion she belonged to, and so her decision to become a Catholic was a gift to my father, a most generous act of love and reconciliation. And so I was finally able to tell a satisfying, if not exactly happy, religious story.

Following are 4 writing prompts to help you tell stories in which religion plays a significant role

For the ***first***, tell a story about religion that exemplifies your particular faith tradition at its best. Start with a list and head it "Being Catholic" or "Being Jewish" or "Being Methodist" and so on. List scenes and images that describe your experiences of this faith, then choose one to tell a story about.

And then some: Tell a contentious story about religion, one in which you experienced something negative about your religious tradition. Start with some scenes, describe a particular one, then see where that leads you. For instance, I remember sitting in freshman religion class at my all-girls Catholic high school listening to the nun tell us that only Catholics went to heaven. That particular scene opens up to many others having to do with my mixed-faith heritage.

And then some more: Describe someone in your life who is very religious—no matter his or her faith tradition. Think of those instances in which this person's religiosity has been a positive force in his or her life. Then tell a particular story about him or her, making sure to put in all the good details and examples that illustrate that.

And then just one more: Forgiveness, central to many spiritual traditions, can lead to some pretty dramatic stories about religion. For this exercise, make a list of personal transgressions that you've yet to forgive yourself for. These can be small or big "sins," from shoplifting a pair of socks to betraying someone's confidence to causing someone physical or psychological harm. Pick just one, describe the experience or event, and include what it would take for you to forgive yourself for it.

From the Trenches

Pat writes about how her father's religious faith was tested

My dad was a disappointed man. The blows inflicted by life on many people of his generation—having to drop out of college to work, delaying marriage because of the depression, losing friends in WWII—all seemed to defeat him more than most. And the fact that his parents were both orphans may have made him less secure about his worth and his place on this earth. So despite being intelligent to the point of being pedantic, my dad never felt he got the recognition or job promotions he deserved. Both he and his brothers ended up in safe jobs in large bureaucratic organizations which they continually complained about but were afraid to leave.

Dad's Catholic religion was his bedrock. He continued to believe that there actually existed a secret about the end of the world revealed to three children in Fatima, Portugal in 1917, long after most other people forgot about it. When Pope John XXIII was elected in 1958, Dad was elated with his promise to open the window of the church and let fresh air in. He learned words like *ecumenism* and *aggornia-mento*. But as the Second Vatican Council convened, his delight turned to dismay. Change after change dismantled the structures and belief systems that had, in so many ways, held him together, and he began to fragment. I remember him literally weeping, saying, "Why can't they leave me alone?"

Dad died two years later. And while the death certificate read cancer, I believe the loss of his religious anchor, something that a more robust personality would have survived, contributed as well.

TRANSITION STORIES

Stories about specific events can usually be found at the major transition points in our lives: births and deaths; love and marriage (and, alas, divorce); school and work; and major moves.

A helpful way to recall these important moments, and tell stories about them, is to take each transition category and list the specific events under them.

For instance, my births and deaths list would include the births of my nieces and nephew, and of their children; my mother's premature death from cancer; my first true love's death in Vietnam; and even the loss of special pets. Then I would choose one entry on this list and begin to write all of my memories about it.

For this ***exercise***, take each of the following transition categories and list all of the specific events under each. Be sure to include not only your own experiences, but those of others that have considerably affected you. (For example, on the moves list, I'd include both my own major moves and those of friends and family.)

- births and deaths
- love and marriage (and re-marriage)
- school and work (including military service)
- major medical events
- significant moves

Over time, you can then select the different specific events from each list and write all of the memories related to it. For instance, from my school and work list, I'd pick "Returning to Graduate School at age 41." Then I'd describe in no particular order all of the experiences, images, and scenes associated with this very interesting transition in my life. From that writing, I'd then choose a couple of stories to record in more detail. And so on.

Remember to keep adding to your lists—not only the transitions you continue to recall from the past, but also those from the present. This way, you'll always have transition stories to tell.

Technology Stories

In 1982, having quit yet another mind-numbing, soul-destroying job, I was hired as the word processor for a gubernatorial campaign. Adlai Stevenson III was running for governor of Illinois, my friend was his campaign office manager, and IBM word processors were the latest in advanced technologies. But I'd neglected to tell Susan during our interview that I'd never used a word processor before; instead I emphasized how fast I typed (90 wpm); what a good Democrat I was (I was); and how badly I needed the job (oh, did I).

When I arrived at campaign headquarters on my first day of work, I suddenly got very nervous. I'd never used anything more complicated than an electric typewriter, and had no idea how to operate the big bulky thing—and all its component parts—sitting dead center in my tiny windowless office.

But the techno-gods smiled down on me that first day: the printer had arrived broken and couldn't be replaced for a week. That gave me the time I needed to plow through Book I of the two volume instruction manual; even better, I used those life-saving days to become fast friends with every one of the tech support staff on the 1-800 help line.

And though I managed over the next several months to become a quite proficient word processor, I never did warm to the technology, reluctant as I was—and still am—to shed my Luddite ways.

Following are 3 writing prompts to help you find your technology stories

For the ***first***, describe an experience when you first started using a piece of technology that you were totally unfamiliar with. This might include a laptop, DVD player, iPod, Cuisinart, cell phone, and so on. Start with a list of those devices, then select one to tell a story about.

And then some: Write about some technology that you resisted for a long time, then finally embraced. Put that item at the top of the page (e.g., Blackberry), then start writing all of the related images that come to mind both before and after you acquired it. See if any of those images lead you to a particular memory featuring that item. For instance, I recall the event that finally got me to buy a cell phone. It was Christmas Day, 2004, and I was bound for a family celebration in California. But the plane I was on had technical problems and we sat on the tarmac for five hours. I had to keep borrowing passengers' and flight attendants' cell phones throughout that nightmare to keep my waiting family alerted.

And then one more: Tell a story about an experience where technology failed you—or at least caused you some sleepless nights.

Stories About Money

Money is a funny thing, especially as the love of it is purported to be the root of all evil. Well, maybe yes, maybe no, but surely the getting, spending, and losing of money can make for some interesting stories.

One of my favorite money stories has to do with when I was newly self-employed. I was in the midst of arranging to teach a journal writing workshop at a women's health spa. Nancy, the owner, was enthusiastic and we picked a day to hold it. Then without hesitation, Nancy asked, "Carol, how much money do you want to make for teaching the workshop?" I could tell by the sound in her voice that she knew what *she* wanted to make to host it.

At first I was speechless, then finally mumbled "I dunno."

No one had ever asked me that question before; they simply told me how much I'd be paid. In the ensuing silence, Nancy told me the dollar amount she expected for providing the space, then suggested what we should charge. By the time she finished crunching those numbers, I knew what I'd be making—which was not the same as what I *wanted* to make.

That conversation took place 15 years ago, yet I still have a clear image of where I was sitting in my apartment during it, the time of day it was, what Nancy said, and, most important, what I didn't. That memory puts me in mind of how complicated the whole money business can be—and the interesting, sometimes charged, stories it can lead to.

Following are 4 writing prompts to help you tell your money stories

For the ***first***, make a list of your experiences that involve money in some central way—getting it, negotiating for it, spending it, finding it, losing it, arguing over it, worrying about it, luxuriating in it, hoarding it. Choose the three most interesting experiences on your list, then describe the most important of those.

And then some: In 1979, while riding the Career Train to Nowhere, I took a job as the dining room manager of a popular restaurant in downtown Chicago. The owners said they'd provide onsite training, but first I'd have to spend several weeks hosting, a job that involved keeping long lines of aggravated people happy.

When those several weeks ended up being months, I finally confronted the owners; they then confessed that there was no manager position in the offing. So I quit, and, on a lark, filed for unemployment compensation, stating I was hired under false pretenses. I was stunned when the claim was approved and weekly checks started showing up in my mailbox. I suppose I should have been thrilled, but to be handed money without expending any effort seemed more than my blue-collar genes could handle. And so long before my claim ran out, I started working for a temp agency.

For this exercise, think about similar experiences in your own life, ones where you felt some disconnect between the money you received and what you did—or didn't do—to earn it. Tell one of those stories.

And then some more: Tell a story about when and how you made a really smart money move, or were pretty crafty in the handling of money. Include how this benefited you and/or others.

And then just one more: Tell somebody else's money story, someone whose way with money you envy, admire, or resent.

Current Events Stories

On Monday evening, September 10, 2001, I started teaching a six-week nature writing course at an artists' retreat north of Chicago. The Ragdale House was built in 1897, and sits on 55 acres of original prairie, including a semi-formal garden. It was the perfect marriage of place and purpose.

As first sessions go, it was pretty typical. We sat around the comfortable antique-laden living room, 12 adults, all talking about our interest in nature and in writing. Then following some brief exercises, our meeting ended and we headed out into yet another beautiful late summer evening.

And when we awoke the next morning, the world had changed.

Along with everyone else in the country, I spent the next week in shock, obsessed with the news, unable to read, think, or talk about much else but the terrorist attacks. But also like everyone else, I had to work and that included returning for week two of the writing workshop.

As I sat on the crowded commuter train headed north, I

wondered if anyone would show up. Or would most now think the workshop pointless, even self-indulgent.

But everyone did come back. And we spent a good part of the evening quietly talking about how both being in nature—and writing about our experiences there—now mattered more than ever. Each experience, we felt, would give us the solace we craved during this time of incomprehensible loss.

Following are 2 writing prompts to help you recall current events that have special meaning for you

For the ***first,*** begin with a list of those events, and be generous with your definition of "current." (I reached back seven years to tell mine.) Think about those public events here and around the world that engaged your interest and/or directly affected your life. These can be happy, sad, scary, or silly events. Choose one event on your list and use the following questions to help you describe it in more detail. When was it? Where were you? Who else was involved? What happened? What effect did it have on you?

And then some: Usually we share with others the impact of major current events. For instance, on the afternoon of 9/11, I was able to finally reach my dear friends in New York by phone, one of whom worked just blocks from the World Trade Center. I often tell her story about that unprecedented event, as well as my own.

Think of the people—friends, family, neighbors—who were a part of a significant current event in your life. Start writing all the images you have of them related to this event. See if a particular memory emerges, then go on to describe it in more detail.

Lessons Learned (Thanks Dave!)

I didn't learn much in kindergarten, and even less from my cat. As with most people, my major life lessons poured in the old-fashioned way: I made plenty of mistakes—often repeating the same ones; I failed, sometimes miserably, when trying to reach important goals; and I didn't always know how to handle life's inevitable setbacks. But I'd like to think that through it all, I managed to pick up a useful thing or two:

- many obstacles really are opportunities;
- learning on the job is unavoidable;
- life gets interesting when we say "yes" more often than "no";
- progress in many things consists of two steps forward and three back;
- telling the truth—especially to oneself—is better than lying;
- telling our stories is a healing process.

Of course, each of these lessons comes with its own story or stories. For instance, when I first started teaching writing 20 years ago—to college freshman at a local university—I was humbled by the difficulty of the task. But, as a result of my years in the classroom, I did pick up one really important lesson: do more of what works and less of what doesn't. And while I first implemented this maxim when responding to my students' writing; I found it applied to just about every aspect of life.

Following are 4 writing prompts to help you tell your "lessons learned" stories

For the ***first***, make a list of the lessons you've learned in your life so far. Be generous with your list—include the very small as well as the really big lessons. Then pick one of the entries on your list, and write down in random order those scenes and images associated with the lesson. See if one of those images leads to an interesting story.

And then some: Learning a lesson may involve our having previously hurt or slighted someone, especially those closest to us—family and friends. Make a list of your family and friends, living and dead, past and present. Then pick one person who helped teach you—perhaps inadvertently—a valuable lesson. Record the details of how that happened.

And then some more: Ask family members and friends how they came to learn one of their valuable lessons, then tell one of the more dramatic of those stories.

And then just one more: I love inspirational quotes, particularly those that are clearly the result of hard-won lessons. Some of these quotes are from famous people, others from those I've met up with in real life. A favorite comes from a previous landlord. When I rented an apartment in his building, I was a bit exercised about all the things that were wrong with it. "Don't worry," he said calmly, "most things, including people, can be fixed."

For this exercise, make a list of your favorite inspirational quotes from the ordinary people in your life, then pick one to write about. Include all the pertinent details: who this person is, what the circumstances of your meeting were, of your hearing the quote. What do you know—or can you surmise—of the story behind it? For instance, I know that my landlord had emigrated from Eastern Europe and had managed, despite many set backs, to "fix" what he needed to in order to survive, even thrive, in his adopted country.

Chapter 6

SUMMING UP...AND KEEPING IT UP

As you work your way through this book, you'll start to accumulate lots of stories worth saving. Now the challenge is to organize them in a way to easily retrieve them. And how you do that will depend on your reasons for writing down these stories in the first place.

Journal writers writing mainly for themselves will want to regularly cull their journals and file away what they want to keep. These are the personal stories you'll want to read again and again for your own pleasure (and illumination).

I keep all my personal journal entries in manila file folders, the accordion kind that expand to hold lots of paper. Each file is then labeled by year. This is surely the roughest way to organize the material, but I plan next to index the significant events from each year, type up that list, and keep it in the year's folder. That way, if I want to read about my ill-fated move to Santa Fe in 1988, or the trip to New York for New Year's Eve in 1994, or what happened on the days immediately following 9/11, I can easily put my hands on those entries.

People writing or contributing to family histories also need to keep files of the stories they are recording. These can be organized as journal files or by project, as with those kept by writers and artists. I'd suggest keeping them as journal files until you type up your stories to share with others.

Once you do that, you'll want to create more specific files, such as "Dad Stories" or "Stories From When We Lived on Birchwood St.," or "Our Family Vacations." I had one student who was writing a family history organized as a series of life lessons for his son. His writing files were provisional chapter titles, and included "Family Traditions," "The Importance of Friends," and "Achieving Success," among others.

I'm about to embark on my own family history project, a little home-grown biography of my great-niece—with particular emphasis on all the adventures we've had together. I plan to give this to her when she turns 21. She's 12 now, so I've a couple more years to wrestle this thing into shape. But at least the beginnings of it—those journal entries kept while it was happening—are safely stashed in bulging manila folders starting in 1995, the year she was born. Once these different stories are typed up in draft form, I will arrange them in chronological order and put them in a manila file marked "Nellie Stories."

No matter the length of your family history project—a story here and there or a whole book (often self-published)—you should devise a system that makes it easy for you to open a drawer, whether on your computer or in a real live file cabinet, and find what you're looking for. There's no right or wrong way to do this. It all depends on what seems logical to your purposes.

Creative writers and other artists who are plundering their lives for raw material will want to organize their stories by project. I write memoir, personal essays, and the occasional service article, and many of my stories find their way into my writing (vs. journal writing) files. These are kept in a separate file drawer and labeled by writing project, usually by essay, article, or book chapter title.

Beginning memoirists interested in writing book-length memoirs will need to first decide on what specific time, theme or aspect of their lives they want to write about. Unlike autobiographies—which chronicle an entire life—memoir focuses on a particular part or feature of it: one's work or profession; parenthood; widowhood; owning a dog; living abroad; dealing with illness. The possibilities are endless.

If you don't already know the focus of your memoir, doing the exercises in this book should help you discover it. And that discovery process will continue as you begin to write the book. That's the nature of writing, after all—it changes even as we are in the middle of it.

As for the organization or structure of your memoir, it should be considered provisional at first, but will get clearer the more you keep writing. During that process of uncertainty, it might be a good idea to create a "working" table of contents. That can help you see what's shaping up to be the book's overall direction and theme. Should that change over time, as it indeed might, your working TOC will also change.

Finally, as this book is not intended to be a step-by-step process for writing a book-length memoir, I've included in the bibliography several how-to guides for that express purpose. These, along with others you may run across, may be helpful as you proceed through the challenging, albeit rewarding, process of writing a book.

Those in the helping professions might want to keep a list of—or simply flag in this book—those exercises that seem especially productive in eliciting personal stories from their clients. It's likely that any exercise dealing with family, or those about holidays, transitions, or loss will evoke meaningful memories. (As Flannery O'Connor once said, anyone who survives childhood has enough to write about for the rest of his or her life.)

Keeping It Up, Part I

Many of this book's exercises have helped you tell stories from the past. From this point on, you can begin recording your present stories, using the techniques from Chapter 2 to get you started. The significant events exercise is especially useful for this purpose.

For instance, I recently returned from 10 days in Ireland, my first trip abroad, and don't yet know which of my adventures I want to write about in more detail. But I kept copious notes in a small memo book while there, especially the names of the people and places we met up with along the way. When I got home, I made a list of the highlights from each travel day, e.g., "Sunday, November 5: breakfast at Dublin B&B; train to Galway from Heuston Station (no such thing, we discover, as reserved seats); walk to Jury's from train station; sandwich and pint at Naughton's; wandering mutt visits us at our outside table; discover huge swans later that night on the River Corrib."

The next step is to review these highlights and choose which of my Ireland stories I want to tell.

Of course I keep a personal journal even when I'm not traveling, and write in it at least once a week, often on Sunday as part of my morning coffee and Sunday paper ritual. I start with a list of the important people, places, and events from the past week—the significant events exercise. It's likely that at least one of these "notes" will develop into a more detailed anecdote or story, which I'll save for future reading.

For instance, I wrote a lot about helping prepare my 95-year-old father for his Thanksgiving celebration with the grand- and great-grandchildren. It was his last Thanksgiving, as it turned out, and I'm glad to have the particulars in writing. I may eventually write this up as a family story, or use it in a personal essay I hope to publish.

You'll find your own way to continue recording your life stories—and that will likely take some experimenting. The important thing is to make this activity routine, a regular habit. For by now you have discovered that writing down, then reading your stories, then *re-reading* your stories, gives you much pleasure—and perhaps a new perspective.

Keeping It Up, Part II

To remain inspired to write down your stories, I highly recommend reading other peoples' stories, whether first-person essays in magazines and newspapers, or published memoirs and biographies. Even if you don't want to get published, or don't plan to write a family history, reading these stories will deepen your own personal writing practice. You'll find inspiration, ideas, even writing prompts when reading these essays and books, all of which will keep you telling your own stories.

You also might want to attend workshops and seminars that focus on personal storytelling, life writing, and geneaology. Most public libraries now sponsor such programs, and many are low-cost or free. More high schools and colleges also offer these types of adult education programs. Take advantage of whichever ones are in your area. Again, you'll get lots of good inspiration and ideas from these classes, both from the instructor and your fellow students.

Also, you may find that writing in response to art and movies will get you thinking about your own life stories. I remember years ago seeing the movie "Impromptu" with Judy Davis and Hugh Grant, the Hollywood version of the relationship between George Sand, the 19th century French woman writer, and Frederic Chopin. I was so taken by the Sand character, her boldness and unconventional life, that I left the theatre and made my way to a nearby restaurant, ordered up some soup and red wine, and wrote furiously in my journal. I was in search of instances in my own life when I'd taken brave steps, even if they weren't the same as Sand's. That movie took me into my own personal stories, just as music and the visual arts do. Next time you go to a concert, theater, or art exhibit, pay close attention to which of your stories are unleashed in the process. Write those down.

And finally this: If you've created some of your own good strategies for keeping at it, I'd love to hear about them. You can e-mail me through my website www.carollachapelle.com and tell me how they've worked. I'm always looking for new ideas to share with my students.

BIBLIOGRAPHY

Bibliographies may seem a bit quaint these days, what with the internet, Google, and Amazon. Why look at the back of a book for recommended readings when you can easily search the worldwide web for everything you need? Still, if you've enjoyed a certain book, and have come to trust the author's judgment, you'll likely be interested in his or her preferences for further reading.

If that holds true for you and this book (and this author), following are some of my reading recommendations. They include books on writing, journal writing, and memoir writing, as well as those related to storytelling in general. For a more extensive selection of each, please visit your local bookseller, or take a trip on Amazon.

BOOKS ON WRITING

I visited my local chain bookstore last week, and had a look at their writing reference section. The shelves were packed with titles like **Writing for Quick Cash, Novelist's Boot Camp, The First Five Pages**, *and* **Technical Writing for Dummies**—*clearly a little something for everybody. Even some of my own favorites were represented. Below you'll find those, as well as others from my collection, a few of which are classics in the genre:*

The Writing Life, by Annie Dillard, Harper Perennial, 1990.

Writing With Power: Techniques for Mastering the Writing Process, by Peter Elbow, Oxford University Press, 1998.

Writing Down the Bones: Freeing the Writer Within, by Natalie Goldberg, Shambhala, 2006.

The Courage to Write: How Writers Transcend Fear, by Ralph Keyes, Holt Paperbacks, 2003.

On Writing, by Stephen King, Pocket, 2002.

Writing Brave and Free: Encouraging Words for People Who Want to Start Writing, by Ted Kooser & Steve Cox, Bison Books, 2006.

Bird by Bird: Some Instructions on Writing and Life, by Anne Lamott, Anchor, 1995.

The Forest for the Trees: An Editor's Advice to Writers, by Betsy Lerner, Riverhead Trade, 2001.

The Faith of a Writer: Life, Craft, Art, by Joyce Carol Oates, Harper Perennial, 2004.

How to Write: Advice & Reflections, by Richard Rhodes, Harper Paperbacks, 1996.

One Continuous Mistake: Four Noble Truths for Writers, by Gail Sher, Penguin, 1999.

If You Want to Write: A Book about Art, Independence and Spirit, by Brenda Ueland, Graywolf Press, 2007.

On Writing Well, 30th Anniversary Edition: The Classic Guide to Writing Nonfiction, HarperCollins, 2006.

Books on Journal Writing

This afternoon, I searched for journal writing books on Amazon, mostly to make sure the ones I'm recommending are still available. The number of titles that came up is pretty amazing. Still, I'm sticking with those I've relied on over the years of teaching journal writing workshops. They include:

The New Diary, by Tristine Rainer, Tarcher, 2004.

One to One: Self Understanding Through Journal Writing, by Christina Baldwin, M. Evans and Company, Inc., 1991.

Life's Companion: Journal Writing as a Spiritual Quest, by Christina Baldwin, Bantam, 1990.

The Well-Being Journal, by Lucia Capacchione, Newcastle Publishing Company, 1989.

The Creative Journal: The Art of Finding Yourself, by Lucia Capacchione, New Page Books, 2001.

At a Journal Workshop, by Ira Progoff, Tarcher, 1992.

Writing to Heal: A Guided Journal for Recovery from Trauma and Emotional Upheaval, by James Pennebaker, New Harbinger Publications, 2004.

Journal to the Self: Twenty-Two Paths to Personal Growth, by Kathleen Adams, Grand Central Publishing, 1990.

A Trail Through Leaves: The Journal as a Path to Place, by Hannah Hinchman, W.W. Norton & Company, 1999.

Books on Memoir Writing

This list includes both "how-to" guides for writing a memoir—many of which I've seen in bookstores but haven't yet read—and books that describe and analyze memoir as a particular kind of narrative nonfiction.

The Situation and the Story: The Art of Personal Narrative, by Vivian Gornick, Farrar, Straus and Giroux, 2002.

Unreliable Truth: On Memoir and Memory, by Maureen Murdock, Seal Press, 2003.

Writing the Memoir: From Truth to Art, by Judith Barrington, The Eighth Mountain Press, 2002.

Your Life As Story, by Tristine Rainer, Tarcher, 1998.

Writing Life Stories, by Bill Roorbach, Story Press, 2000.

How To Write Your Own Life Story: The Classic Guide for the Nonprofessional Writer, by Lois Daniel, Chicago Review Press, 1997.

Write From Life: Turning Your Personal Experiences into Compelling Stories, by Meg Files, Writer's Digest Books, 2002.

You Don't Have To Be Famous: How to Write Your Life Story, by Steve Zousmer, Writer's Digest Books, 2007.

Almost There, by Nuala O'Faolain, Penguin Books Ltd, 2004. (This is itself a memoir, but contains many useful comments about the form in general.)

Other Books of Interest

Both as a writer and teacher, I'm keenly interested in the human impulse to tell stories, across all cultures and time. Why do we seem to need stories so much? How are all the ways they nourish us? Who would we be or become without knowing our stories? The following books attempt to answer these questions.

Kitchen Table Wisdom: Stories That Heal, by Rachel Naomi Remen

Bibliography

Stories We Live By: Personal Myths and The Making of the Self, by Dan McAdams, Ph.D.

Your Mythic Journey, by Sam Keen

The Call of Stories, by Robert Coles

The Healing Power of Stories: Creating Yourself through the Stories of Your Life, by Daniel Taylor, Ph.D.

The Seven Basic Plots: Why We Tell Stories, by Christopher Booker